The Passages of Thought

THE PASSAGES OF THOUGHT

Psychological Representation in the American Novel 1870–1900

GORDON O. TAYLOR

NEW YORK
Oxford University Press
1969

Library of Congress Catalogue Card Number: 74-75608

Printed in the United States of America

for Tatiana

Acknowledgments

Henry Nash Smith has given generously of his knowledge and time during all phases of my work on this book. I am deeply grateful for his continued interest, for the benevolent firmness of his criticism, and for the many ways in which the precision of his ideas has worked toward the clarification of my own. Richard Poirier read the manuscript in an earlier form, and has kindly assisted me with important suggestions regarding its method and substance. My wife Tatiana has given me persistent encouragement toward completing this project, and the benefit of her keen editorial eye during preparation of the manuscript. I wish also to express my appreciation to Whitney Blake, Editor at Oxford University Press, and to Laura Johnson, of the Oxford editorial staff, for valuable counsel and courteous assistance.

G.O.T.

Cambridge, Massachusetts
February, 1969

Acknowledgments

Contents

The Passages of Thought

Introduction

By what strange law of mind . . . ?
HARRIET BEECHER STOWE,
Uncle Tom's Cabin (1852)

It is not for us, who only tell what happened, to solve these mysteries . . .
OLIVER WENDELL HOLMES,
The Guardian Angel (1867)

Now, it has been shown experimentally . . .
THEODORE DREISER,
Sister Carrie (1900)

One feature of the general shift in the form and direction of American fiction during the late nineteenth century is a marked change in novelists' assumptions about the nature of psychological process. This is accompanied by a comparably marked change in the degree to which novelists rely on psychological analysis as central to the representation of experience in a fictive world. The techniques through which psychological representation can function as a substantive or structural element of fictional narrative undergo corresponding transformations. This book is an attempt to describe these changes, as they occur in particular ways within the developing art of particular writers, and—in the sense of broad tendency rather than of linear progression—over the period 1870–1900.

In deciding which novelists are most clearly relevant to such an attempt, and which of their novels most clearly embody this relevance, I have been primarily concerned with discerning patterns of change in what I shall call "fictive psychology," rather than making judgments about intrinsic literary value or upholding traditional distinctions between "major" and "minor" figures. I consider, however, that such patterns are of some importance in relation to the more general change in the shape and aim of the American novel, and do not simply constitute a secondary current outside the mainstream. I have therefore chosen to examine these patterns in the work of five of the most important writers of the period: Henry James, William Dean Howells, Stephen Crane, Frank Norris, and Theodore Dreiser.[1] I have chosen to describe the patterns as they appear and emerge in several of the best known and most representative novels by these authors: *Roderick Hudson, The Portrait of a Lady,* and *The Ambassadors* by James; Howells's *A Modern Instance, The Rise of Silas Lapham,* and *A Hazard of New Fortunes;* Crane's *Maggie: A Girl of the Streets* and *The Red Badge of Courage; McTeague* by Norris; and Dreiser's *Sister Carrie.* The book begins, however, with a discussion in Chapter 1 of James's *Watch and Ward* and Howells's *A Chance Acquaintance.* These early efforts are viewed against a background of established convention represented by Harriet Beecher Stowe's *Uncle Tom's Cabin.* The book concludes, similarly, with a consideration of Norris and Dreiser, also both at the beginning of their careers, against the background of literary change observed in the intervening chapters.

Understood in relation to an individual novel, the term "fictive psychology" has several facets. We must first consider the novelist's psychological assumptions as they can be inferred from his text and seen as a set of related ideas about the mind and its workings. The relation between these assumptions and the novel's premises or values more broadly viewed must be examined to see whether the writer's psychological notions function smoothly or produce friction within his conceptual framework. Overlapping these considerations are the ways in which the novelist uses the techniques of fiction—diction and imagery, characterization, devices for representing specific mental processes, point of view, narrative method, resolution of fictive issues—to make his psychological assumptions operative in the fictive world. We must also recognize and differentiate the various problems which arise when techniques based on the novelist's original assumptions are not supple enough to carry new concepts of mental processes into full fictive operation. The relation of such problems to actual change in the psychological technique of the novel will be one of our principal concerns.

Thus, the analysis of fictive psychology in a single work or in a group of novels spanning a period encompasses two main topics: the author's premises concerning the nature of the mind, and his embodiment of these premises in fictive art. Since any novel contains some sort of fictive psychology, whether or not its author avows psychological interests, such analysis also provides a basis for comparative discussion of works differing widely in style, theme, and values.

Roughly between 1870 and 1900 fictive psychology in the American novel undergoes a fundamental shift which may be summarized as follows. The basic view of the mind underlying the representation of consciousness in fiction moves away from a notion of static, discrete mental states requiring representational emphasis on the conventional nature of particular states, toward a concept of organically linked mental states requiring representational emphasis on the nature of the sequential process itself. At the beginning of the period, writers generally focus on a single level of rational awareness and develop it as conscious, logical introspection on the part of the character. As the period progresses, a broader and more complicated spectrum of psychological experience appears in their work, containing instinctual and sub- or semiconscious levels or bands. At the close of the period, writers generally focus on links between interior process and exterior behavior in characters who are no longer introspectively aware of movement or change within their own minds. At the beginning the basic frame of reference for psychological representation is abstractly moral; it assumes that mind is non-physical, and measures the narrative importance of a mental event by its relation to the moral values and issues of the novel. At the end of the shift this frame of reference has become concretely environmental; mind is assumed to be physiological, and the development of narrative as well as the shaping of fictive issues depends on its response to environmental stimuli.

Mind as an adjunct of "soul," a moral lens through which abstract values are focused to order the facts of the fictive world, gives way to mind as "brain," a specialized organ seeking an accommodation with those facts. In the former case, abstract values resolve psychological (generally synonymous with moral) conflicts, and are themselves the prime reality in the fictive world—more real than the facts over which they have control. In the latter case, psychological processes encounter and explore conflicts between abstract values and facts which no longer submit to their control. Environmental problems and the changed concept of mental process now comprise the prime reality with which fiction sets out to deal. As interest in interior process becomes more important to the narrative thrust of the novel, and more intimately connected with the writers' changing conceptions of the "real," psychological representation requires new techniques. Therefore, the shift results in technical developments aimed at intensifying and extending analysis of the mind in process, and at building this analysis more centrally into the narrative flow of the novel.

A comparative examination of two passages will illustrate this summary of literary change, as well as demonstrate my method of analysis. I shall not deal exhaustively at this point with the fictive psychology of either work; the passages have been chosen for maximum contrast, and the analyses are intended simply to sink methodological supports for the ensuing chapters firmly in the tissues and textures of fiction.

The first passage is from Stowe's *Uncle Tom's Cabin* (1852) and provides an example, perhaps extreme, of conventional nineteenth-century practice in fictive psychology.[2] At the beginning of Chapter 12, as the slave-trader Haley and the slave Tom (whom Mr. Shelby has just sold to Haley in settlement of a debt) ride toward the boat which will carry Tom "down river," Mrs. Stowe makes the following psychological observations:

> Mr. Haley and Tom jogged onward in their wagon, each, for a time, absorbed in his own reflections. Now, the reflections of two men sitting side by side are a curious thing,—seated on the same seat, having the same eyes, ears, hands and organs of all sorts, and having pass before their eyes the same objects,—it is wonderful what a variety we shall find in these same reflections!
>
> As, for example, Mr. Haley: he thought first of Tom's length, and breadth, and height, and what he would sell for, if he was kept fat and in good case till he got him into market. He thought of how he should make out his gang; he thought of the respective market value of certain supposititious men and women and children who were to compose it, and other kindred topics of the business; then he thought of himself, and how humane he was, that whereas other men chained their "niggers" hand and foot both, he only put

> fetters on the feet, and left Tom the use of his hands, as long as he behaved well; and he sighed to think how ungrateful human nature was, so that there was even room to doubt whether Tom appreciated his mercies. He had been taken in so by "niggers" whom he had favoured; but still he was astonished to consider how good-natured he yet remained!
>
> As to Tom, he was thinking over some words of an unfashionable old book, which kept running through his head, again and again, as follows: "We have here no continuing city, but we seek one to come; wherefore God himself is not ashamed to be called our God; for he hath prepared for us a city." These words of an ancient volume, got up principally by "ignorant and unlearned men," have, through all time, kept up, somehow, a strange sort of power over the minds of poor, simple fellows, like Tom. They stir up the soul from its depths, and rouse, as with trumpet call, courage, energy, and enthusiasm, where before was only the blackness of despair.[3]

Mrs. Stowe first notes that both men are physiologically similar and perceive the same external environment, but explicitly points out that these facts have no real importance in the psychological narrative. Physiology consists randomly of "eyes, ears, hands and organs of all sorts," with brain presumably one of the latter. Physical reality consists of the "same objects" passing before their eyes, although Tom's fetters represent a huge difference in physical circumstances. The irony of these lines confirms the irrelevance of such considerations when we discover Mrs. Stowe's real subject. She is not interested in her characters' reflections as mental processes except insofar as they dramatize, by sharp contrast, a moral difference between the two men. The reader has already been made aware of this difference, and is assumed to be in agreement with the author concerning it.

A narrator, indistinguishable from the novelist herself, reports several thoughts from Haley's mind, all in the form of conscious introspection. These thoughts are weighted equally through even punctuation, and represent aspects of a single mental state—smug, calculating, self-righteous satisfaction—of which Mrs. Stowe has previously instructed the reader to be morally critical. No sense of organic sequence emerges. A faint hint of such sequence appears in the movement from considering "market value" to thinking about "humanity," which, however, has meaning only in terms of Haley's respect for quality merchandise. But this has little narrative value compared with the static moral portrait begun earlier when Haley first appeared in the story. A trace of *erlebte Rede,* or use of the character's idiom in a third-person statement recording his mental process, appears in the word " 'niggers' " and in the absence of the otherwise consistent "he thought" from Haley's final idea. By setting Haley's epithet off from the formal diction and elaborate periods with which she controls the passage, Mrs. Stowe minimizes the idiomatic flavor and hence the element of direct representation. The thought remains formally attributed to the character's mind, rather than represented directly from it.

Tom has a single, recurrent thought, also consciously introspective, which is that of the inspiring scriptural lines. Though they keep "running through his head, again and again," he remembers them, and Mrs. Stowe quotes them, directly from the Bible, suggesting that his mental repetitions are significant not as an independent process but as a fixed moral lens. This lens concentrates the force of an unchanging spiritual reality on the malleable facts of the physical situation, even those as harsh as Tom's chains and his eventual death at the hands of Simon Legree. The "strange power" of scripture is not restricted to "the minds of poor, simple fellows, like Tom," nor is it altered by the passage of time. The rigid subordination of psychological analysis to the development of a moral contrast reflects the primacy of Christian values "through all time" over human or terrestrial realities.

The only psychological change suggested in the passage is the potential movement from despair to courage in Tom's "soul," which Mrs. Stowe equates with his "mind." This change is to be accomplished by the "trumpet call" of scripture, instead of by a process originating within Tom's mind. The "depths" of this soul-mind contain the only possibilities implied here for more complex levels of awareness, but they remain undeveloped and are more clearly associated with the morally negative quality of despair. As a psychological event with moral significance, Tom's anticipated response to the trumpet call is the narrative end-in-view of the whole sequence. As psychological process, however, it requires less textual space than the summary, for moral purposes, of Haley's thoughts.

Nothing discovered by a character or revealed to the reader, then, depends on sustained psychological scrutiny. Mrs. Stowe's moral assumptions, which are not themselves subject to fictive inquiry, control both thematic emphasis and structural proportions in the sequence. Given these assumptions and the ways in which they account for psychological mechanics, more varied or direct representational methods are unnecessary.

This passage marks our point of departure; the second, from Dreiser's *Sister Carrie* (1900), indicates our destination. Chapter 33 introduces Dreiser's prolonged concern with the degeneration of George Hurstwood, with whom Carrie has been living in New York since they fled Chicago together. This thread extends through the rest of the novel, with Hurstwood's fall and final suicide counterpointing Carrie's success. The following passage exhibits the psychological premises of this portion of the novel, and demonstrates their role in its development:

> During all this time—a period rapidly approaching three years—Hurstwood had been moving along in an even path. There was no apparent slope downward, and distinctly none upward, so far as the casual observer might have seen. But psychologically there was a change, which was marked enough to suggest the future very distinctly indeed. This

was in the mere matter of the halt his career had received when he departed from Chicago. A man's material progress is very much the same as his bodily growth. Either he is growing stronger, healthier, wiser, as the youth approaching manhood, or he is growing weaker, older, less incisive mentally, as the man approaching old age. There are no other states. Frequently there is a period between the cessation of youthful accretion and the setting in, in the case of the middle-aged man, of the tendency toward decay when the two processes are almost perfectly balanced and there is little doing in either direction. Given time enough, however, the balance becomes a sagging to the grave side. Slowly at first, then with a modest momentum, and at last the graveward process is in the full swing. So it is with man's fortune. If its process of accretion is never halted, if the balancing stage is never reached, there will be no toppling. . . .

Hence, some men never recognise the turning in the tide of their abilities. It is only in the chance cases, where a fortune or a state of success is wrested from them, that the lack of ability to do as they formerly did becomes apparent. Hurstwood, set down under new conditions, was in a position to see that he was no longer young. If he did not, it was due wholly to the fact that his state was so well balanced that an absolute change for the worse did not show.

Not trained to reason or introspect himself, he could not analyze the change that was taking place in his mind, and hence his body, but he felt the depression of it. Constant comparison between his old state and his new showed a balance for the worse, which produced a constant state of gloom or, at least, depression. Now, it has been shown experimentally that a consistently subdued frame of mind produces certain poisons in the blood, called katastates, just as virtuous feelings of pleasure and delight produce helpful chemicals called anastates. The poisons generated by remorse inveigh against the system, and eventually produce marked physical deterioration. To these Hurstwood was subject.[4]

A "psychological change" immediately appears as the key to the reader's understanding of a tendency in Hurstwood which the "casual observer" in the fictive world cannot yet see, and of which Hurstwood himself has no introspective knowledge. Psychological analysis will thus provide the reader with his main access to the fictive "future," and is Dreiser's main task as he begins to develop this element of his plot. Hurstwood's movement "in an even path" does not refer to his mental condition, in which change is more "marked," but to his apparent physical well-being and visible behavior. Dreiser conceives of mind, too, in terms of motion and organic process, and as being closely related to physiology and environment.

Indeed, his first approach to the details of Hurstwood's psychology is a reference to change in the character's physical and social situation, "the mere matter of the halt his career had received." As the passage proceeds, Dreiser shows that the mental impact of this change is far from "mere," and establishes in his analysis the idea of mind as primarily sensitive to environmental conditions. He pursues this notion through a triple analogy among "material progress," "bodily growth," and mental capacity. All three are subject to constant processes of strengthening and weakening, and the last two are virtually synonymous. "There are no other states" apart from these processes, and even the "almost perfect balance" between opposing forces gradually changes over time. The passage of time itself is crucial here, because it brings about conditions and actions respectively influencing and reflecting interior changes. This implies the observation from without of mental events, and confirms the importance of such events in the passage of *fictive* time, or basic narrative movement. Conceptions of balanced forces and momentum in mental processes, together with diction such as "cessation of . . . accretion," extend the suggestion of observation from without by connoting scientific detachment.

In the first paragraph, Dreiser lays a foundation of what amounts to psychological theory for his actual narrative of Hurstwood's mind. In the second, he focuses directly on that mind. "Chance" and "new conditions," having removed Hurstwood from the success which shielded him from an awareness of his physical and mental decline, are clearly the main stimuli to psychological change. Dreiser links bodily processes with mental ones here, since the basic reality toward which he is leading Hurstwood's perceptions is essentially a physiological fact: "that he was no longer young." Waning mental capacity and inability to cope are, as much as simple aging, the subjects of this latent discovery. Discovery is latent because Hurstwood's condition is still balanced enough to prevent him from consciously observing change. More importantly, it is latent because the mental experience which interests Dreiser most is sub- or semi-conscious instead of introspective. This experience is also bound up with fictive behavior—the speech and action through which the story moves. In this sense, the entire passage is a theoretical foundation from which Dreiser will trace the results of Hurstwood's interior change through the rest of the novel.

"Not trained to reason or introspect himself" suggests at first that conscious self-analysis by the character would be appropriate if Hurstwood possessed skills assumed to be natural in *Uncle Tom's Cabin.* That Dreiser does not assume this is significant, but even more so is the nature of the "introspection" for which Hurstwood lacks specialized knowledge and which Dreiser—a detached analyst possessing such knowledge—explains to the reader. The "change which was taking place in his mind, and hence his body" (the equation recalls by contrast the one between mind and soul in *Uncle Tom's Cabin*) is not a conscious train of thought but a biochemical process influencing the direction of conscious thought. Each phase of the process occurs and makes an impact before it can be perceived subjectively, and introspection in the conventional sense is irrelevant. Hurstwood's awareness of his worsening circumstances leads to mental depression, which in turn produces "poisons in the blood." These poisons result in "physical deterioration," which continues the cycle and underlies Hurstwood's degeneration at plot level. Hurstwood, as a fictive character, is "subject" to this process; that is to say Dreiser must account for it in describing his actions. The process itself, though structurally important, is "subject" to Dreiser's Darwinian assumptions about the nature of reality, just as mental process, which is structurally unimportant to Mrs. Stowe, is controlled by her commitment to Christian reality.

The novelist's references to psychological "experiment" and his use of the technical terms "katastates" and "anastates" indicate an interest in the relevance of theoretical psychology to fiction. Whether or not his technical knowledge is accurate, and whether or not the experiment he cites is real or imagined, he brings formal theory into a narrative already focused on mental process. Thus, psychology is present as subject matter, as well as relevant to Dreiser's representational technique. All this is found, moreover, in a novel which does not set out, any more than does *Uncle Tom's Cabin,* to be an esoterically "psychological" work.

The words "virtuous" and "remorse" suggest the persistence of moral considerations in Dreiser's fictive psychology. Their moral resonances jar slightly in this non-ethical context, but they fit into the general patterns of the passage. "Virtue" emerges as physical well-being, and Hurstwood's "remorse" and eventual suicide (suicide having its own moral resonance in earlier literary conventions) are not moral reactions but cause and effect in a psychophysical process. Because Hurstwood is mentally unfit, he cannot survive physically any more than the morally unfit Legree can survive spiritually. Similarly, the frequent use of the word "state" pulls slightly against the notion of organic change, but Dreiser clearly emphasizes the movement from one psychological state to another. Nevertheless, these hints of unresolved tension between so basic an aspect of style as diction and the assumptions shaping overall narrative indicate a problem in fictive psychology with which we shall be centrally concerned.

In one sense, a comparison of these passages shows little change in representational method. In both, author and third-person narrator are closely identified. Indeed, Dreiser is even more intimately omniscient of mental events than is Mrs. Stowe, mainly because of the increased importance of psychological detail. Much of this passage is a theoretical lecture, analogous in point of view to Mrs. Stowe's moralistic and theological commentary. Even the final portion of Dreiser's passage is an authorial explanation of what he will later develop dramatically, although it has elements of more direct psychological narrative. Dreiser, unlike certain of the other writers considered in this book, is not interested in creating techniques for representing the mind without his overt intrusion. He is interested, however, in using the techniques at hand to integrate psychological analysis with the themes as well as the narrative structure of his novel, and in this sense the technical difference between Mrs. Stowe and himself is basic and extensive.

On the basis of these model analyses, the questions comprising the central undertaking of this book may now be posed more precisely. What seem to be the major sorts of literary change connecting these polarized examples? What are the phases and nuances of change, and what are the elements of continuity? What are the characteristic qualities—or difficulties—as fictive psychologists of the novelists who are most relevant to the discussion of such movement? How do older conventions break down, and how do certain elements of outworn conventions contribute to innovation? What can such a study reveal about the importance of this shift within the more general movement in American literature which Warner Berthoff describes as "the ferment of realism"? [5]

My efforts toward answers to these questions rest ultimately on close, cumulative examination of a group of passages embodying —through a selective schematization—the movement between our models. The arrangement of selected texts is not strictly chronological, since in this literary transformation, as in all others, flow is defined as much by its interior eddies and cross-currents as by its overall direction. Rather, they are drawn from the work of James, Howells, Crane, Norris, and Dreiser, and gathered into clusters forming the substructures of chapters which focus on those writers. Many of the central issues reside within the different conceptual and technical frameworks that emerge from these clusters of narrated thought. There is, nevertheless, a general, although by no means linear, coherence to the larger shift implied in the comparison between Dreiser and Stowe. Without claiming such coherence as an historical absolute, and without attempting to document its motion in relation to other impulses in cultural history, I am concerned with observing the general drift as well as the particular currents of change.

The evidence of the novels themselves, then, is crucial. Biographical information and critical materials are introduced only occasionally, to support rather than to control arguments which depend finally on the analyses of texts. Considerations of broad intellectual history and cultural change, while important to the exhaustive investigation implicit in this exploratory study, remain peripheral here, although their peripheral presence is welcomed. Let us turn to the novels, and to the transformations in fictive psychology—the passages of thought—which they reveal.

ONE

The Hinging-Point of Great Emotions

> She itched gently, she hardly knew where,—was it in heart or brain?
>
> HENRY JAMES,
> *Watch and Ward*

The pattern of fictive psychology observed in the passage from *Uncle Tom's Cabin* provides a point of departure. The real beginning of the shift, however, may be viewed as occurring with the first indications of movement away from that pattern. These may be found in the earliest novels of James and Howells, and I shall focus in this chapter on a work by each, examining the fictive psychologies of both against the background of established conventions apparent in Mrs. Stowe's novel.

James's *Watch and Ward* appeared serially in the *Atlantic Monthly* in 1871 and was published in book form in 1878.[1] Howells's *A Chance Acquaintance* was published in 1873. Each is a first novel, James's literally so, and Howells's virtually so despite the appearance of *Their Wedding Journey* in 1871. (*A Chance Acquain-*

tance grew out of an incident in *Their Wedding Journey* and is conceptually similar to the earlier work, but it contains a more sustained dramatic development and thus can be better compared to *Watch and Ward*.) That both writers preferred to think of other novels as their first—James favored *Roderick Hudson* (1876) and Howells *A Foregone Conclusion* (1875)—enhances rather than diminishes our interest in these earlier books. Because each author, without having fully matured as a novelist, was ready by the middle seventies to write fiction which he considered better and more characteristic than his earliest work, the features of the earliest work are particularly relevant. They represent each writer's heaviest reliance on conventional materials, and constitute the first span of a bridge which leads from such reliance toward the discovery of more distinctive interests and methods, and ultimately to the firm ground of a developed art.

Watch and Ward and *A Chance Acquaintance* provide examples of fictive psychology dependent on and largely accepting conventional premises and techniques, yet imperfectly committed to them and showing potential or actual movement toward new ones. Psychologically these novels share an unformed quality which is the prelude to change, whereas *Uncle Tom's Cabin* is complete in archaic terms and resistant to change. One purpose of this chapter is to indicate the conventional aspects of fictive psychology in both James and Howells at the beginning of their careers. Another is to make certain distinctions between the two, as a basis for separate emphases to be developed in later chapters. A third is to show in each of these books how a fictive psychology susceptible to change contributes directly to a tendency away from the archaic pattern. This will show how ground is being prepared for more substantial innovations in psychological representation. To begin, however, I shall resume the discussion of *Uncle Tom's Cabin* to fill out the conventional background.

When Uncle Tom first appears in Chapter 4, Mrs. Stowe prefaces her initial description by saying that "as he is to be the hero of our story, we must daguerreotype [him] for our readers." The "daguerreotype" in this instance is brief, non-psychological and mainly abstract; Tom is introduced simply as "a large, broad-chested, powerfully-made man, of a fully glossy black, and a face whose truly African features were characterized by an expression of grave and steady good sense, united with much kindliness and benevolence." Beyond this we are told only that his general bearing combines "self-respect and dignity" with "a humble simplicity." The word "daguerreotype," however, is of more direct interest in relation to a study of fictive psychology.

Daguerreotype, the photographic process of Mrs. Stowe's day, differed from modern film photography primarily in the longer time required to fix an image on a chemically coated plate of glass or metal. A clear picture of the subject consequently depended on a well-sustained pose, and the process was naturally more suitable for formal portraiture than for recording spontaneous action. Mrs. Stowe uses the term without special emphasis or deliberately metaphorical intent, in the sense of "describe" or "present." Her choice of the word and simple use of the metaphor, however, seem delibrate, as if she intended to certify in a casual detail the sort of fidelity to objective reality which she claims for the entire work. Yet, throughout the novel, reality is ultimately a matter of Christian values rather than of mundane facts. Here, what is introduced as a photographic likeness of Tom turns out to be, with the exception of a few unremarkable physical details, a reading of his moral character. His face and "air," rather than characterizing him, are themselves characterized by abstract qualities with strong moral connotations. In Mrs. Stowe's interpretation of the literary photograph, these qualities are as real as is his physical presence, and much more important.

The point is not that the novelist misuses the word "daguerreotype," but that the sustained pose required by daguerreotype photography is integral to her narrative technique. Within its own terms, moreover, this aspect of her art is quite sophisticated. In critical scenes involving several characters—such as the deathbed scenes of Augustine St. Clare and Little Eva—as well as in her introductions of key individuals, Mrs. Stowe often creates and holds a "still," formally posed word picture, which she then proceeds to interpret at her leisure. To use another photographic analogy, although one limited by its anachronism, it is as if she stops a motion picture at certain intervals to analyze individual frames for abstract content impossible to convey explicitly through continuous movement.

This tendency toward static portraiture and analysis bears more directly on the fictive psychology of *Uncle Tom's Cabin* when Mrs. Stowe introduces us to Ophelia St. Clare on her arrival in New Orleans. She has journeyed by river boat from Vermont to join the household of her cousin Augustine and to help care for his daughter Eva. The novelist poses her new character before the reader: "Miss Ophelia, as you now behold her, [as she] stands before you. . . ." The sense of the character's complete removal from dramatic context is further heightened because whereas she first "stands before" the reader, when the narrative of actual events is resumed three pages later, "There she is, sitting now in her stateroom" on the boat. During the interval in which Ophelia "stands" for a formal introduction and description, Mrs. Stowe, without actually using the term again, "daguerreotypes" her mind:

> As to mental cultivation,—she had a clear, strong, active mind, was well and thoroughly read in history and the older English classics, and thought with great strength within certain narrow limits. Her theological tenets were all made up, labelled in most positive and distinct forms, and put by, like the bundles in her patch trunk; there were just so many of them, and there were never to be any more. So, also, were her ideas with regard to most matters of practical life,—such as housekeeping in all its branches, and the various political relations of her native village. And, underlaying all, deeper than anything else, higher and broader, lay the strongest principle of her being—conscientiousness. Nowhere is con-

> science so dominant and all-absorbing as with New England women. It is the granite formation, which lies deepest, and rises out, even to the tops of the highest mountains.[2]

The obvious regional satire warns us against taking the passage as a direct index of the author's psychological assumptions. Yet it is not the basic composition but the rigidity of Ophelia's mental labels and bundles that is being satirized. Even in context this satire is incidental. Just as the cubbyholed patch trunk of Ophelia's mind, with its carefully pre-cut and pre-sorted ideas, gives way to the granitic mental bedrock of her conscience, so the satiric content of the passage seems to fade. The basic psychological structure implied in these images—rigid mental compartments containing fixed resources for dealing with experience and supported by a firm moral base—is common to most characters in the novel. In figures more central than Ophelia to Mrs. Stowe's main concerns (and Mrs. Stowe is herself, of course, a "New England woman"), theological tenets assume the same priority over matters of practical life, and conscience is just as dominant and all-absorbing. The sense of rational clarity and control within a single dimension of awareness; the sense of an intellect shaped primarily by tradition; the sense of a moral framework for mental process which is "higher and broader" as well as "deeper than anything else," and thus as fully enclosed conceptually as a patch trunk is physically—these aspects of the passage make this "daguerreotype" of Ophelia's mind emblematic of Mrs. Stowe's fictive psychology.

A passage concerning a mental process which occurs within the narrative of actual events, and confirming the pattern of assumptions contained within this abstract emblem, appears considerably later in the story. Cassy, a once-beautiful quadroon whom Legree's brutality has worn down and brought to despair, has resisted Tom's efforts to bring her the solace of Christian faith. She is so embittered by her experience as a slave that she can "only hate and curse" when she tries to pray, and Tom, fearing for her soul in such morally destructive circumstances, urges her to escape. Unable to trust in God for deliverance from the swamp and Legree's bloodhounds, Cassy knows "no way [to escape] but through the grave." Yet she responds to Tom's calm faith in "Him that saved Daniel in the den of lions," and to his pledge to pray for her:

> By what strange law of mind is it that an idea long overlooked, and trodden under foot as a useless stone, suddenly sparkles out in new light, as a discovered diamond?
>
> Cassy had often revolved, for hours, all possible or probable schemes of escape, and dismissed them all, as hopeless and impracticable; but at this moment there flashed through her mind a plan, so simple and feasible in all its details, as to awaken an instant hope.
>
> "Father Tom, I'll try it!" she said, suddenly.
>
> "Amen!" said Tom; "the Lord help ye!" [3]

The word "strange" recalls the "strange sort of power" Holy Writ holds over Tom's mind in the passage discussed in the Introduction. It suggests that the "law of mind," in its interest for the novelist and its importance for her narrative, remains subordinate to the law represented by her religious values. The causal force of these values within the fictive world, a force exerted in the model passage by the "trumpet" of scripture, is exerted here by prayer. In context, it is Tom's absolute faith in the efficacy of prayer which precedes and seems to release the idea "long overlooked" in Cassy's mind. His final "Amen!" suggests that Cassy's decision to escape is more important as a confirming sign of this efficacy than as a purely psychological event. Viewed in this light, the strangeness of mental processes derives primarily from their links with the mystery of God's purpose concerning all human experience, rather than from their intrinsic complexity. Mrs. Stowe therefore asks a rhetorical question about the strange law of mind instead of making an analytical statement about it. Whether or not she intends to imply a theological answer, she requires no answer at all to keep the narrative moving. The law of mind itself remains something less than primary subject matter in the passage, and receives no direct analysis.

Within this theological frame the novelist places an image which is explicitly psychological: Cassy's sudden insight is seen as a "discovered diamond," formerly "trodden under foot as a useless stone." Although presented almost parenthetically, in a rhetorical question about the mind in general and not about Cassy's in particular, this image constitutes an element of psychological analysis more clearly concerned with the mind in process and more directly related to a particular dramatic situation than is the psychological daguerreotype of Ophelia. The form of Mrs. Stowe's question suggests a briefer, less obvious pause in the narrative for purposes of abstract comment. Cassy's discovery is set squarely in the fictive present, in the sequence of immediate events, and it is her own discovery, even if the light which prompts it is shed by Tom's religious faith.

Both the "flash" of a feasible plan of escape in Cassy's mind and her "instant" psychological shift from hopelessness to hope are dependent, none the less, on spiritual light imparted by Tom. This light is both sudden and total—it reveals the most basic realities of Mrs. Stowe's fictive world, relegating less important realities (such as the physical danger to Cassy) to the background, and a character is either sensitive to it in a given situation or he is not. An apparently useless stone will sparkle and be recognized as a diamond only in a changed light, just as the brilliant colors in many rocks are visible to us only under ultraviolet light. Thus, Cassy can accurately see her situation only under the particular moral illumination provided by Tom. Once this illumination occurs, perception is instantaneous, as is the shift to another state of mind. No study of the stone itself is required for its identification since there are no unknown possibilities: it is either common and useless or it is a diamond, and the answer lies not in its crystalline structure but in its sudden sparkle. Thus the novelist focuses on the separate, polarized states of Cassy's mind, without inquiring into the psychological processes which connect them. There are no unknown *psychological* possibilities, no unique mental crystals requiring careful analysis, and the conventionally known quality of "hope" (its outward "flash" rather than its intrinsic design) sends the story forward into the next chapter.

Three other aspects of *Uncle Tom's Cabin* may be quickly mentioned as bearing on the problem of fictive psychology, though all three amplify basic points which have already been introduced. Dreams are less interesting to Mrs. Stowe as psychological phenomena than they are as another means of illustrating the moral qualities of her characters. When Legree dreams it is not his mind but his "bad soul" which enters "the shadowy world of sleep," a "land whose dim outlines lie so fearfully near to the mystic scene of retribution." The account of the dream itself, which culminates when Legree imagines he is falling "down, down, amid . . . shouts of demon laughter," is an acute representation of his guilt. Its main contribution to the narrative, however, is a semi-literal prefiguration of a fully literal damnation, the moral basis for which is already clear to the reader. Tom's dream of Eva, who is dead, reading to him from the Bible and seeming to "rise on shining wings," further illustrates the literal connection between the landscape of dreams and supernatural terrain. Mrs. Stowe explicitly allows the possibility that Tom's dream is objectively real: "Was it a dream? Let it pass for one. But who shall say . . . ?" She then inserts a quatrain which, though intended as a theological grace note, could pass for a theory of psychological mechanics consistent with the novel's values:

> It is a beautiful belief,
> That ever round our head
> Are hovering, on angel wings,
> The spirits of the dead.[4]

The subject of mental aberration, which the author touches on briefly in connection with Cassy, is just as precisely circumscribed in its narrative function as the subject of dreams. Cassy's occasional "raving insanity," the strongest expression of her frustration under the "hideous yoke of her servitude," is mentioned only in a "daguerreotype" still. Mrs. Stowe gives no specific indication of how the processes of an insane mind change, nor does she indicate what insane behavior is in a given situation. The moral connotations of this insanity, although ambiguous, outweigh its importance as a psychological fact. Mrs. Stowe links the aberration with Cassy's inability to pray and her conviction that "I've got the devil in me!"—the devil which Tom fears will overwhelm her if she cannot escape Legree. The same aberration, on the other hand, is simply an excess of righteous anger which contributes, along with the conventional influence of a "strong, impassioned woman . . . over the most brutal man," to Cassy's intermittent moral power over Legree, who has a "superstitious horror of insane persons." [5]

So too, Mrs. Stowe gives no explanation of the "paroxysm" of maternal love which enables Eliza, one of Mr. Shelby's slaves, to escape with her son from the Shelby farm and to prevent the boy's being sold "down river" along with Tom. Like the granitic conscience of Ophelia St. Clare, Eliza's mother-love is "stronger than all," a substratum of conventional rock upon which the psychology of the entire scene is based. "It seemed to [Eliza] as if strength poured into her in electric streams"—the metaphor differs strikingly from the static conceptions characteristic of the novel. "Electric streams" at first suggest a fluid, continuous process, a physical current generated by maternal instinct. Electricity can be as sudden as the sparkle of a diamond, however, and this current is ultimately more theological than psychological. Eliza's prayers frame the scene just as Tom's prayers frame the one in which Cassy decides to escape. Eliza's thoughts during her flight are dominated by a sense of a "supernatural power that bore her on," and "that was no part of her." A "supernatural tension of the nervous system" accompanies these thoughts, but Mrs. Stowe makes no attempt to incorporate physical or neural processes into the narrative of Eliza's mind. Indeed, she accounts for "that alert perception peculiar to a state of excitement" as "a sort of inspiration." [6] We must not overlook the evidence that Mrs. Stowe makes a strictly psychological observation here—that nervous stress affects perception—and that she is no less able than later novelists to make such a connection. It is the "inspired" quality of Eliza's heightened awareness rather than the mental state itself, however, which bears narrative weight, which fits the psychological observation into Mrs. Stowe's scheme, and which makes it unnecessary for her to elaborate that observation by means of internal analysis.

Thus, diverse portions of the novel, in a variety of ways, bear out the pattern embodied in the model passage from *Uncle Tom's Cabin,* and amplify our conclusions about the book's psychological texture. Mrs. Stowe is not without an interest in the "law of mind," and she is aware of mental process as an aspect of experience which a novelist must account for and may explore. Her methods of doing both are not without sophistication, and are well-suited to her assumptions about the mind. We have also seen, however, that in her fiction psychological analysis is subordinated to moral analysis: abstract values endowed with causal force influence perception directly and often instantaneously, and therefore command more narrative attention than the workings of the mind itself. Since these values are fixed and since the nature of reality is never in doubt, how her characters perceive reality is relatively unimportant. The psychological processes by which they might discover the nature of an unknown or changed reality, a reality which their original values cannot define or control, are completely irrelevant.

Such processes seem no more relevant in *Watch and Ward* or *A Chance Acquaintance* when these works are viewed in their entireties. Certain aspects of these novels, none the less, show James and

Howells edging toward a fictive psychology in which the drama of awareness is more central.

James's handling of the first scene in *Watch and Ward*—Roger Lawrence's encounter with Mr. Lambert—indicates a basic similarity between the patterns of psychological assumption and representation in this work and in *Uncle Tom's Cabin.* The scene begins as Lawrence sits in the drawing room of his hotel, awaiting the appointed hour of his final, futile proposal to Isabel Morton. We have not yet been told about the nature and background of his relationship with her. The scene is preceded only by James's initial description of Lawrence, which is similar in its abstraction and moral orientation to Mrs. Stowe's "daguerreotype" of Uncle Tom, though somewhat richer in physical detail. Indeed, James poses Lawrence for this description by having a hypothetical observer, who is "less superficial than the majority" and who is able to address the reader directly, ask, "Have you ever studied his face?" Such a study reveals nothing specific about Lawrence's mind; it tends rather to suggest a conventional character-type—the gentleman-hero "with a tender heart, and a genius, almost, for common sense"—whose values and role are familiar enough to preclude intensive narrative concern with his mental processes. Lawrence's encounter with Lambert is therefore the reader's introduction to the former as a character engaged in a particular situation, and to how James portrays the psychological aspect of this engagement.

In response to the sudden appearance of Lambert, a total stranger whose "whole aspect was that of grim and hopeless misery," Lawrence "smoothed down his lavender gloves, watched him and reflected":

> "What an image of fallen prosperity, of degradation and despair! I have been fancying myself in trouble; I have been

dejected, doubtful, anxious. I am hopeless. But what is my sentimental sorrow to this?" [7]

The glove-smoothing composure of Lawrence's reflection contrasts sharply with the external signs of Lambert's agitation—violent movements, audible groans, burying face in hands—the description of which constitutes James's only analysis of Lambert's state of mind. Here as in *Uncle Tom's Cabin,* to reflect is to introspect, consciously and in terms of separate states or images rather than in a sequential flow. Thus, as Lawrence walks toward Isabel's home shortly afterward, having refused to give Lambert a hundred dollars and having been "shocked and discomposed" by Lambert's angry rejection of an offer of ten, the "image of his heated petitioner was speedily replaced by the calmer figure of Isabel Morton." In Lawrence's initial reflection formal diction, rhetorical phrasing, and even alliteration emphasize a sense of his conscious control over his own thought, within the broader frame of the author's omniscient reporting of it. In language and structure, as well as in representational technique—direct quotation—Lawrence's thought process is indistinguishable from his actual conversation, which in turn is not far removed stylistically from the novelist's narrative voice.

Lawrence's sense of shock and discomposure has no effect on either the conscious level or the measured formality of his mental processes. In itself it is not a subject of psychological interest to James and he makes no effort to examine it in detail. It is the direct and uncomplicated result of Lawrence's "brutal collision with want and vice" in the person of Lambert, whose moral transgressions are inferred from his obvious need. Thus, shock and discomposure are aspects of a reaction which we discover, as the scene develops, to be basically moral instead of psychological in its interest for James and its relevance to his narrative. The charity of Lawrence's first response to Lambert is tempered by a sense of "something horribly disreputable in his manner," and James represents the psychological sources of decision and action on Lawrence's part in a form resembling moral allegory:

> He of course had no imagination, which, as we know, should always stand at the right hand of charity; but he had good store of that wholesome discretion whose place is at the left. Discretion told him that his companion was a dissolute scoundrel, who had sinned through grievous temptation, perhaps, but who had certainly sinned. His misery was palpable, but Roger felt that he could not patch up his misery without in some degree condoning his vices.[8]

Even though James takes an ironic view of his hero on occasion, he means the moral concern underlying Lawrence's decision to be taken seriously. This concern proceeds from values which, though less comprehensive than the explicitly Christian values of *Uncle Tom's Cabin,* are none the less real in James's fictive world, and which play an important role in its ordering. The novelist is of course also solving a purely technical difficulty in this opening scene: Lawrence must refuse Lambert so that Lambert will have reason to commit suicide, providing Lawrence with the opportunity of becoming the guardian of Lambert's daughter Nora, and providing James with the relationship which is his real subject. Lambert's suicide also makes sense on moral grounds, since the notion that he is a dissolute scoundrel is never seriously challenged, and even to his daughter he is a safer object of filial emotion "now [that] he can do no harm." Lawrence consciously and permanently dismisses the idea that he is responsible for the suicide, and James expects the reader to do likewise.

Nora herself, throughout much of the novel, is a prime example of a conventional character-type—the innocent heroine—in whom automatic moral reflexes tend to replace mental activity, thus minimizing the author's concern with psychological representation. When she becomes Lawrence's ward at the age of twelve, James refers to her as "an unknown quantity" and "an unsolved problem." She is a piece of uncut ivory from which Lawrence, a Jamesian Pygmalion, will try to carve his Galatea. Nora, however, is actually the focus of the novel's system of values from the outset. Her innocence, like Uncle Tom's faith, is an unquestioned *donnée,* a quantity known to writer and reader alike, and a source of power over her world rather than of vulnerability before it. Like Ophelia St. Clare's conscience, Nora's innocence is "the strongest principle of her being," a principle by which James can account for most of her motives and reactions without resorting to internal analyses of her thoughts.

Consider, for example, a brief scene between Nora and her cousin George Fenton which occurs in the final chapter. Nora has come to New York from Boston to find work and achieve "perfect independence" after discovering that Lawrence has brought her up in the hope of marrying her, and that he somehow expects her consent in return for his pains even though he has no intention of forcing it. She has sought temporary refuge with her cousin, innocently mistaking his purely financial interest in her for genuine friendship. Fenton once hoped to marry Nora for the money he expected Lawrence to settle on her, but now he plans to demand a handsome sum from Lawrence in exchange for persuading Nora to return to him. Her innocence has created the situation, but it also constitutes an infallible moral instinct which enables her to perceive and control the situation without any psychological representation on James's part:

> That George deliberately lied Nora did not distinctly say to herself, for she lacked practice in this range of incrimination. But she as little said to herself that this could be the truth.[9]

Admittedly a mental event is implied: although innocence prevents her from fully recognizing one of Fenton's many lies, Nora easily senses an element of falsehood. But conventional values are the real agents of perception, and she does not need to think (or rather to "distinctly say [anything] to herself") for the benefit of narrative. The psychological influence of her moral intuition extends to the minds of other characters with whom she is involved. Fenton feels self-contempt when he is in Nora's vicinity, and James has only to expose him to the "chilling blast of [her] reprobation" to bring about Fenton's most penetrating insight: "O Lord! I am an ass!"

There are other suggestions in *Watch and Ward* of a fictive psychology essentially similar to Mrs. Stowe's. When Nora returns from a year in Europe to find Lawrence seriously ill, she seems to "apprehend as by a sudden supernatural light" the extent of his kindness toward her. To Lawrence himself, earlier in the story, it seems "that he had obeyed a divine voice" in deciding to adopt Nora. Language such as this does not refer to controlling values as pervasive as those in *Uncle Tom's Cabin,* but it serves a representational purpose similar to Mrs. Stowe's. In the same way, the vocabulary of formal logic often characterizes James's accounts of his characters' thoughts, without referring to an intellectual system methodically worked out in the novel as a whole. And while James devotes considerable narrative attention to Nora's "expansion" from child into young woman, he conceives of the psychological aspect of this change as the abrupt "dismissal" of the "mental pinafore of childhood," a process involving the exchange of one pre-designed mental garment for another.

Midway through the final chapter, however, James refers to another sort of psychological expansion in a statement which represents something fundamentally new in our discussion, although the idea is not borne out in this work as a whole:

> It is strange how the hinging-point of great emotions may rest on an instant of time. These instants, however, seem as ages, viewed from within. . . .[10]

Cassy's instantaneous perception—the external flash of a mental diamond—relieves Mrs. Stowe of the need to account for whatever strange internal process may be involved. Here James is suggesting that "an instant of time" can be the "hinge" of a more complex and extended psychological process, that this instant has intrinsic narrative possibilities, and that the key to these possibliities lies in "viewing from within" the character's mind. James too finds such questions "strange," but he is beginning to find them more directly relevant to his fiction than they ever become in Mrs. Stowe's. Although in this early novel awareness to him is mainly a matter of the single "reverberating moment" (a phrase appearing later in the passage just quoted), rather than of a cumulative succession of moments, he is beginning to develop an interest in psychic reverberations for their own sake.

In *Watch and Ward* just how embryonic and ineffective this interest is may be seen in the passage immediately after Nora, having read a letter written much earlier by Lawrence which says in part, "It will be my own fault if I have not a perfect wife," realizes the true nature of his intentions toward her:

> Nora frequently wondered in after years how that Sunday afternoon had worked itself away; how, through the tumult of amazement and grief, decision, illumination, action, had finally come. She had . . . [made] her way half blindly to her own room, had sat down face to face with her trouble. Here, if ever, was thunder from a clear sky. Her friend's disclosure took time to swell to its full magnitude; for an hour she sat, half stunned, seeming to see it climb heaven-high and glare upon her like some monstrous blighting sun. . . . The whole face of things was hideously altered; a sudden horror had sprung up in her innocent past, and it seemed to fling forward a shadow which made the future a blank darkness.[11]

James focuses retrospectively on Nora's mental "tumult" (a static condition in this context, despite the word's connotation of movement), which comes from the instantaneous "spark" of insight that "flashed back over the interval of years." The process by which this insight "swells to its full magnitude" to become a total state of mind is at the center of James's interest. Nora's realization "took time," and the metaphor of a sun rising in the sky and increasing in intensity bears out this notion. Awareness, moreover, has "hideously altered" her world. The conditions of her existence have changed, and the psychological processes involved in discovering and exploring new conditions are now important to the story. A conventional resolution disposes of the problem because Nora slips easily into the role of "perfect wife" at the end. But for the moment when she discovers the letter reality is beyond her conventional control, her moral antennae have failed her, and she stands in need of a mind with which to try to cope with her changed situation.

James's effort in this passage to give her such a mind, and to view her situation "from within" it, produces an archaic effect none the less. The idea of perception as a thunderclap, a "sudden horror," counters his sun image, and the random sequence of "decision, illumination, action" further restricts the germinal concept of organic process. Not even Nora can see things from within. She must run to her room, which seems to become a necessary extension of her mind whenever she has to think, and "sit down face to face" with a personified "trouble." (James elsewhere describes her eyes as having a "soft introversion of their rays," a phrase suggesting concentration on internal processes but also suggesting the conventional introspection by means of which he is able to report her thoughts from without. At one point Mrs. Stowe refers to Little Eva's eyes in similar terms.) Nora is not equipped, nor is James at this stage, to explore this problem in psychological terms. She sits thinking for an hour, but it is really an hour-long "instant," during which she remains stunned by a single psychic shock. James is beginning to realize that the reverberations of such a shock might be rich in narrative potential, but he is unable yet to tap it. Even as she leaves for New York, Nora is recovering the use of the moral radar which is part of her conventional role, and which will guide her safely past Fenton and back to Lawrence without any sustained analysis of her mind by James.

Because the novelist has not really endowed his heroine with a mind having narrative substance of its own, and because he is moving toward a kind of fiction which will require such minds of its central characters, the future which now seems a "blank darkness" to Nora must remain a psychological blank to the reader. Conventional fictive psychology fills the blank, just as a conventional ending returns Nora to a well-lit and familiar future. But we are left with the sense of an opportunity missed in this novel, and an interest in how James will handle similar opportunities in later works.

Latent possibilities for the exploration of consciousness are also discernible in the fictive psychology of *A Chance Acquaintance,* but for the most part they are even more fragmentary and more tightly restricted than those in *Watch and Ward.* When Howells introduces Kitty Ellison, the heroine of this novel, she is sitting on the promenade deck of a steamer moored in the St. Lawrence River off Quebec, "letting her unmastered thoughts play as they would in memories and hopes around the consciousness that she was the happiest girl in the world." A faint suggestion of unconscious or at least involuntary process appears in "unmastered," but it is Kitty who allows her thoughts to "play as they would," and she retains a conscious mastery over her perceptions. Moreover, her ideas play inconsequentially and in generalized categories "around" the single, simple mental state that is the focus of the sentence, instead of constituting a train of thought, however incidental, leading toward or beyond that state.

Howells, of course, is simply making an introductory observation here, and it is unlikely that he would immediately attempt an extensive analysis of his heroine's mind even if he had more explicit psychological interests to explore in the novel. Brief as it is, however, the observation suggests a basic pattern with which we are by now quite familiar, and which is borne out in the novel along lines already discussed in connection with James and Mrs. Stowe. Consciousness in *A Chance Acquaintance* is primarily conscientiousness (Howells uses the terms interchangeably on occasion), an automatic sensitivity to clear-cut moral values and the values governing clear-cut roles. Introspection, which is morally oriented, is the character's habitual mode of thought. The author's habitual means of representing thought is as an omniscient narrator-commentator, who imposes his own language and rhetorical style on the character's mind.

The workings of Kitty's mind figure in Howells's narrative mainly in connection with her romance with Miles Arbuton, a young man representing the "mysterious prejudices and lofty reservations" of Boston society. She meets him during a trip on the St. Lawrence with her cousins, Colonel Ellison and his wife Fanny. Arbuton is attracted to Kitty, and she sees in him "that divine possibility which every young man is to every young maiden." The novel has "begun like a romance," and the ready-made reactions of romantic hero and innocent heroine call for little in the way of psychological analysis throughout the first half of the story.

Kitty, however, who comes from a small town in New York, finds Arbuton's social rigidity and esthetic dogmatism increasingly disturbing, though her romantic interest in him persists. The complex distinctions and judgments of his world represent something new in her experience. Howells casts Arbuton's values in a distinctly negative light, and endows Kitty with an intuitive mistrust of them similar to Nora's mistrust of Fenton in *Watch and Ward*. For each young woman this mistrust is a moral reflex which the novelist simply assumes at certain points without actually representing it as a mental process. For Howells, the problem is basically the same in its psychological aspect as that recognized, but not dealt with, by James in *Watch and Ward*. This is the problem of representing a character's mental encounter with a more complicated kind of experience than that which she is conventionally accustomed to, of registering in narrative form an internal change which may take her beyond the previous limits of her role. The following passage contains Howells's nearest approach in *A Chance Acquaintance* to direct treatment of such an encounter and such a change:

> . . . Then there was a silence, while she brooded over the whole affair of her acquaintance with Mr. Arbuton. . . . It had begun like a romance; she had pleased her fancy, if not her heart, with the poetry of it; but at last she felt exiled and strange in his presence. She had no right to a different result, even through any deep feeling in the matter; but while she owned, with her half-sad, half-comical consciousness, that she had been tacitly claiming and expecting too much, she softly pitied herself, with a kind of impersonal compassion, as if it were some other girl whose pretty dream had been broken. . . .
>
> "Sometimes, Fanny," she said, now, after a long pause, speaking in behalf of that other girl she had been thinking of, "it seems to me as if Mr. Arbuton were all gloves and slim umbrella,—the mere husk of well-dressed culture and good manners. His looks *do* promise everything; but O dear me! I should be sorry for any one that was in love with him." [12]

Although Kitty is with Fanny in the latter's room, and not alone in her own, a prolonged silence suspends all action for the duration of her introspective broodings, confirming a kinship between this passage and others which Howells frames more explicitly as conscious "reveries" or "meditations." Elsewhere, indeed, Kitty goes to her room to confront the "mists of her own trouble," just as Nora goes to hers to face a similarly externalized trouble. (In at least one episode in each book the heroines' writing desk, at which she "steadies herself" to think, also serves as a physical extension of her mind.)[13]

Kitty's immediate problem is a growing awareness that a relationship which had begun like a romance is not developing according to romantic plan, and the psychological effect of this awareness is her feeling of "strangeness." Howells means this term to express her sense of "exile," of surprise at feeling herself a stranger, at times, to Arbuton. The novelist himself, however, also finds the sensation "strange," and only vaguely definable, just as James and Mrs. Stowe refer to certain aspects of the mental process as strange. In *Uncle Tom's Cabin* the "strange law of mind" is only peripherally relevant to the main concerns of the author; here, as in *Watch and Ward,* the word "strange" is potentially something more than a simple description of a mental process. It suggests once again the possibility of more direct fictive inquiry into the nature of the view from within, and of increased interest in this view as a source of narrative material and momentum.

Howells distinguishes between Kitty's "fancy," the romantic imagination to which the conventional "poetry" of her suitor's attention appeals, and her "heart," a deeper center of romantic commitment which Howells has never quite allowed to become fully engaged in her relationship with Arbuton. Neither of these faculties, however, constitutes a mind which would be capable of critical awareness of the situation, nor of processes which would lead toward such awareness. "Heart" seems on several occasions in the novel to function essentially as a synonym for mind, as does the word "soul" in *Uncle Tom's Cabin.* But the workings of Kitty's heart-mind are controlled largely by the conventions of a romantic love-plot, or by the protective moral instinct which Howells has given her without representing it as thought. In the same way, the workings of Uncle Tom's soul-mind are controlled by absolute and pervasive religious values. In neither case is there an intrinsic mental process other than the sort which Mrs. Stowe represents as the "sudden sparkle" of a diamond, James as the "flash" of a "vital spark," and Howells as a "heat-lightning flash." [14] Howells is at least implicitly confronted in this passage, however, with the problem of showing the gradual development of a basic conflict within Kitty's mind, a conflict produced by an increasingly obvious flaw in the "pretty dream" of romance.

He responds to the problem by externalizing the conflict through the figure of the "half-sad, half-comical" masks of traditional theater, and in effect creates a second heroine with a different type of mind. Kitty "owns" (a word with characteristically conscientious overtones) to herself that love is turning out to be more complicated than she had imagined, but Howells delegates her capacity for full awareness of this to "some other girl," a second Kitty whom she can pity with "impersonal compassion" for having lost a pretty dream, without experiencing the loss herself. And, when the silence of her introspection is broken, it is "that other girl she had been thinking of" whom Howells permits to draw the relevant conclusion concerning Arbuton: "I should be sorry for any one that was in love with him." Thus a conflict between two distinct sorts of awareness, requiring different sorts of mental engagement, becomes for a moment the focus of Howells's narrative. Even as he introduces this conflict, however, the novelist is setting it aside from his immediate interests by leaving the conflicting element, the "other" view of Arbuton, embodied in a shadowy double of his heroine to whom he will not refer again. The psychologically uncomplicated Kitty remains dominant, and "pities" her imagined double without understanding her; the "other" Kitty is "sorry for" her more romantic counterpart (that is to say, for the heroine as she appears throughout the story), but does not really contend with her for control of the character's perceptions and behavior as the narrative proceeds.

This is because at the level of plot, and in the context of the book's overall action, Howells is by no means yet prepared to break the romantic dream. Kitty's engagement to Arbuton is still a hundred pages away, and she can neither possess the awareness nor act on the decision relegated to her "other" mind until after he proves his shallowness by snubbing her before his society friends and she breaks the engagement. By then Howells has insulated her against the psychic shock of disillusionment. It is as if she had known all along through her protective intuition what she only begins to realize in the passage above, and the fictive psychology of the concluding portion is thoroughly conventional. Even Kitty's thoughts of happiness upon accepting Arbuton's proposal come to mind in curiously conditional terms:

> . . . and she thought that if all were well, and he and she were really engaged, the sense of recent betrothal could be nowhere else half so sweet as in that wild and lovely place.[15]

Her unhappiness, by the same token, is brief and superficial, and Howells gives it little analytical attention.

Thus, it is only in the sequence dealing with Kitty's divided mind that the reverberations of psychological change begin to move toward the narrative surface of this novel. Yet neither the mental impact that the broken dream has on Kitty, nor the process by which that impact develops into a conclusion which might be expected to have a fundamental bearing on her stance and behavior, is really studied or integrated with the general action of the work. Howells, like James in *Watch and Ward,* is beginning to sense the relevance to his fiction of such considerations, but he cannot yet handle psychological complexity in terms of the individual mind. He can only imagine the conflict as a polarity which occurs instantly and exists temporarily between two separate minds that, like the masks of theater, belong to different ways of envisioning and telling a story. He can resolve the conflict only by setting Kitty's "other" mind, with its latent interior view of the situation, safely apart from the main development of his story.

Howells's early fiction, like Kitty's relationship with Arbuton, has "begun like . . . romance," and has shifted briefly and tentatively in the direction of something else before being resolved (despite the departure from the conventional marriage formula) along essentially romantic lines. A shift of essentially the same sort occurs in the fictive psychology of *Watch and Ward.* Each novel reaches a point at which the author's representation of a character's mind seems to be based on slightly altered assumptions, or seems to become slightly more central to the unfolding of narrative. This "hinging-point," to use James's phrase, creates or implies a new kind of representational problem. The nature of each writer's interest in this kind of problem, and the particular directions in which he pursues his interest, become clear only in his later works. Neither novelist really recognizes the problem at this stage, although James is closer than Howells to an awareness of the narrative possibilities of the "view from within."

Leon Edel's remark that *Watch and Ward* reflects an "imagination not yet free, not yet master of itself, not yet fully responsive," [16] might apply to *A Chance Acquaintance* as well. This chapter has been largely concerned with showing that the imaginations of James and Howells are not yet free of certain conventions in their earliest attempts to portray the mind in process. Tracing the progress of these and other writers toward their respective sorts of mastery in psychological representation, as well as trying to show what they become more fully responsive to as they develop in this aspect of their art, will be the business of the chapters that follow. In these novels both James and Howells, if only momentarily, have found conventional means of representing the mind inadequate. Since neither is yet in control of new methods or free of the old the result is a small but noticeable "blank" in the fictive psychology of each work. Following the passage in which Howells bisects his heroine's mind, Kitty remarks to Fanny "what a curious story" her experience with Arbuton would make, and then inadvertently comments on the difficulty of telling such a story in its psychological entirety at this point in the development of the American novel:

"Then, why don't you write it, Kitty?" asked Mrs. Ellison. "No one could do it better."

Kitty flushed quickly; then she smiled: "O, I don't think I could do it at all. It wouldn't be a very easy story to work out." [17]

Two

The Friction of Existence: Henry James

The common and constant pressure . . .
The Ambassadors

In the autumn of 1870, when he was still at work on *Watch and Ward,* James wrote to J. T. Fields of the *Atlantic Monthly* to assure him that the story would prove to be "one of the greatest works of 'this or any age!' "[1] Whether prompted by conviction or semi-ironic salesmanship, this judgment was short-lived, and after the appearance of *Roderick Hudson*—serially in the *Atlantic* in 1875 and in book form in 1876—James began to refer to his second novel as his first. His preference in the matter was lifelong, and in the preface which he wrote in 1907 for the New York Edition of *Roderick Hudson*[2] he called the book "my first attempt at a novel, a long fiction with a 'complicated' subject." Having thus disowned *Watch and Ward,* or at least denied it the saving grace of a " 'complicated' subject," and having at the same time offered a broad definition of the novel as a literary form, James goes on to discuss the general nature of "complexity" in the novel. What he terms "developments" or "relations" among the people, events, places, and things in a work of fiction, the varicolored filaments which bring selected points on the "canvas of life" into a rich and coherent pattern, are the elements of Jamesian "complication":

> [Relations] are of the very essence of the novelist's process, and it is by their aid, fundamentally, that his idea takes form and lives; but they impose on him, through the principle of continuity that rides them, a proportionate anxiety. They are the very condition of interest, which languishes without them; the painter's subject consisting ever, obviously, of the related state, to each other, of certain figures and things. To exhibit these relations, once they have all been recognised, is to "treat" his idea, which involves neglecting none of those that directly minister to interest. . . .
>
> Really, universally, relations stop nowhere, and the exquisite problem of the artist is eternally but to draw, by a geometry of his own, the circle within which they shall happily *appear* to do so.[3]

Once drawn, James continues, this circle "remains in equilibrium by having found its centre, the point of command of all the rest":

> From this centre the subject has been treated, from this centre the interest has spread, and so, whatever else it may do or may not do, the thing has acknowledged a principle of composition and contrives at least to hang together.[4]

I quote James at this length because the "geometry" by which he attempts to draw such a circle in *Roderick Hudson,* the "centre" from which he attempts to command the relations within that circle, and indeed the "principle of continuity" or of "composition" to be found in the relations themselves, all bear directly on the question of change in his fictive psychology. Only at the end of

Watch and Ward, and then only incidentally, does James refer to the "view from within," although he seems to glimpse the possibilities inherent in such a view earlier in the novel. It is as if the phrase itself could not occur to him until after he had stumbled upon a particular problem of psychological representation which remained inaccessible or "blank" to the view provided by conventional fictive psychology. *Roderick Hudson* embodies from the start a deliberate (if not wholly successful) effort on James's part to view an entire fictive action from within the mind of a central observer who is himself dramatically involved. Moving on in his preface from the portions quoted above, he writes:

> The centre of interest throughout "Roderick" is in Rowland Mallet's consciousness, and the drama is the very drama of that consciousness—which I had of course to make sufficiently acute in order to enable it, like a set and lighted scene, to hold the play. By making it acute, meanwhile, one made its own movement—or rather, strictly, its movement in the particular connexion—interesting; this movement really being quite the stuff of one's thesis.[5]

To be sure, James wrote the preface more than thirty years after he first published the novel, and well after he had developed his theory of relations far beyond the stage represented by *Roderick Hudson.* We cannot assume that his view of the story in 1907 is identical with his view of it in 1875, nor can we use the language of the preface as our primary base for an analysis of his original conception. Indeed, the notion of the movements of a character's consciousness as the "centre" of interest in a novel, the basic "stuff of one's thesis," seems more fully and accurately relevant to James's latest works, particularly *The Ambassadors,* than to *Roderick Hudson.* Nevertheless, the novel of 1875 bears out the substance of James's retrospective analysis in the preface. Even though it fails in complete artistic implementation of these ideas, it shows a significant increase in the concentration of James's psychological interests beyond the point represented by *Watch and Ward*. The novelist himself concedes in the preface that these interests are not fully realized, "not really *worked-in,*" so that the fabric of the novel remains a "pale embroidery" psychologically speaking, as well as in other respects. "Whatever else it may do or may not do," however, the fictive psychology of *Roderick Hudson* constitutes a foundation—more complex and more susceptible to organic development than that provided by *Watch and Ward*—upon which James goes on to build, in later works, a specialized and distinctive mastery of psychological representation.

In this chapter I shall describe the movement in his fiction through which he does so: movement toward firm control and full artistic use of a concept of narrative in which the processes of a character's mind are centrally "interesting," and which therefore acknowledges the representation of mental process as its basic "principle of continuity." I shall examine first the emergence of the pattern in *Roderick Hudson,* then the extension and refinement of it in *The Portrait of a Lady* (1881), and finally its culmination in *The Ambassadors* (1903). This will produce a sense of the range of development and change in James's fictive psychology, though of course it will neither account completely for transitional detail nor catalog fully the special problems posed by other James novels.

The consciousness of Rowland Mallet, a young bachelor of ample means with a keen esthetic sense and leisure for frequent sojourns in the art capitals of Europe, seems at first to be cast in a familiar mold. The central figure of *Roderick Hudson* if not the titular hero, he initially strikes us as similar in appearance and demeanor to Roger Lawrence in *Watch and Ward,* and his mind also appears to be a simple extension of his moral sense. James suggests on the first page that it will be an important "part of the entertainment of this narrative to exhibit [that] Rowland Mallet had an uncomfortably sensitive conscience." He also tells us early on that Rowland, like Roger, "took life in [a] conscious, serious, anxious fashion," a phrase which recalls Howells's reference to Kitty Ellison, who is examining her thoughts in the "close-curtained space" of her room, as a "puzzled, conscientious, anxious young girl."

We soon suspect that more complicated assumptions about the nature of the mind than those embodied in James's earliest fiction are at work here. Rowland's moral cast of thought is partly attributed to his "primal Puritan" antecedents instead of silently assumed, and is in partial conflict with other facets of his mind: "His was neither an irresponsibly contemplative nature nor a sturdily practical one. . . . He was an awkward mixture of moral and aesthetic curiosity." James does not necessarily conceive of the moral and the esthetic as opposites, but his "awkward mixture" of the two in Rowland's mind suggests the possibility of internal mental frictions, of subtler and more continuous psychological tensions, than we have yet discussed.

James amplifies this suggestion by hinting that Rowland's mind is perhaps less sensitive to the demands of conscience or the influence of abstract values than to another kind of friction, the "friction of existence" in a world where such values are no longer absolute. The phrase is neither emphasized nor elaborated in this novel; like the phrase "viewed from within" in *Watch and Ward,* however, it has implications which extend far beyond its immediate context. In a general sense, the "friction of existence" implies the continuous modification of one's perceptions by one's experience, an abrasive action resulting from a continuous relation between the workings of a particular mind and the situations comprising that individual's experience. Thus, it suggests a tendency toward an environmental frame of reference for psychological representation. In a related but slightly different sense, the phrase implies a disparity between one's conscious assumptions about the nature of reality and the actual conditions governing his existence, a disparity inevitably producing psychological friction. This suggests a tendency toward fictive emphasis on the processes which sharpen or alter one's awareness of reality by wearing down one's illusions. James will develop these tendencies in his later novels, and then only in certain characteristic ways. However, an important door has been opened in his fictive psychology (an opening door or window comes to be one of James's favorite psychological images), and in *Roderick Hudson* he begins to explore the chambers into which it leads.

Before leaving Boston to spend the winter in Rome, Rowland visits his cousin in Northampton, Massachusetts. Here he meets Roderick Hudson, a young sculptor. He recognizes Roderick's talent and is drawn to him even though temperamentally they are "as different as two men could be." Rowland wants to rescue Roderick from his law studies, to take him to Rome to extend his intellectual and artistic horizons. Roderick eagerly accepts, and before his departure becomes engaged to Mary Garland, a serious, quiet girl to whom he is "everything" but to whom Rowland is secretly attracted. In Rome Roderick immerses himself in antiquities and new impressions and feels himself subtly changed, almost physically different. Early in Chapter 5 he discusses this feeling with his companion:

> "What becomes of all our emotions, our impressions," he pursued after a long pause, "all the material of thought that life pours into us at such a rate during such a memorable three months as these? There are twenty moments a week—a day, for that matter, some days—that seem supreme, twenty impressions that seem ultimate, that appear to form an intellectual era. But others come treading on their heels and sweeping them along, and they all melt like water into water and settle the question of precedence among themselves. The curious thing is that the more the mind takes in, the more it has space for, and that all one's ideas are like the Irish people at home who live in different corners of the room and take boarders."

> "I fancy it's our peculiar good luck that we don't see the limits of our minds," said Rowland. . . . "That belongs to youth; it's perhaps the best part of it. They say that old people do find themselves at last face to face with a solid blank wall and stand thumping against it in vain. It resounds, it seems to have something beyond it, but it won't move. That's only a reason for living with open doors as long as we can.[6]

The principal difference between the basic views of consciousness in *Watch and Ward* and *Roderick Hudson* is apparent in this passage. Unlike the "electric streams" with which divine providence steels Eliza's mind at a moment of crisis in *Uncle Tom's Cabin,* and unlike the allegorical debate through which abstract morality creates a decision in Lawrence's mind at the outset of James's earlier story, "the material of thought" is poured by life itself into the minds of Roderick and Rowland in a constant, cumulative flow. James has by no means excluded abstract concerns from his notion of life, but the kaleidoscopic variety of physical reality has become an equally basic source of psychological stimulus.

Individiual "emotions" or "impressions" are recognizably separate, but only in a transient sense. Instead of producing completely distinct states, they soon merge "like water into water" with the fluid sequence of which they form a part. The "question of precedence" among them depends less on the conscious moment than on the continuity of that sequence, and on the relations which develop among moments of consciousness as the sequence progresses. The pattern of relations is itself fluid, and subject to change in the light of continuing experience. Ideas cannot be permanently sorted, bundled, and boxed, like the patches in Ophelia's mental "trunk"; nor can an "intellectual era," such as that represented by the "mental pinafore" of Nora's childhood, be completely discarded and left behind. Instead, both individual impressions and entire mental stages shift into new relations to one another as time passes and the mind expands.

James suggests both the fluidity of immediate consciousness and the flexibility of the mind by means of images which show a conceptual advance from those in *Watch and Ward*. In that novel, Nora first imagines the mind of Hubert Lawrence, her guardian's brother, as an "immutably placid and fixed" pool "of lucid depth and soundless volume." As she comes to know him, and senses his romantic interest in her, she sees "ripples" on the surface of the pool, and hears it "beating its banks." The difference indicates a certain capacity for psychological change in both characters. James, moreover, by ascribing the two notions to Nora's mind "of old" and "of late" respectively, seems almost to associate the slight shift in the pool image, as well as the passing of fictive time, with growth over time in his own fictive psychology.[7] The pool, however, remains essentially static—its boundaries remain fixed, and become even more rigid because the waves of Hubert's passion, which threaten briefly to breach them, turn out in dramatic context to be superficial and meaningless. By contrast, in the passage from *Roderick Hudson* the mind is represented as a stream with its own intrinsic motions and variable boundaries. Its flow may "tread on the heels" of preceding impressions, as when a swift current enters a deep, slow-moving pool, or may forcibly "sweep them along," as when the current quickens again when it reaches the pool's outlet. In the pool as well as in the stream—the two have essentially become one—water melts into water, adjusting the momentum of its currents, settling its mental sediments at various rates, refracting light and reflecting objects in ceaselessly changing patterns.

James's idea of the mind as a room or house shows corresponding differences from earlier conceptions. The "close-curtained" rooms in which Nora Lambert and Kitty Ellison do their heavy thinking, and which seem almost necessary extensions of their minds, are related to the more elaborately imagined "three-storey brain" with which Oliver Wendell Holmes endows Clement Lindsay in *The Guardian Angel* (1867). Lindsay, the hero of this novel in which Holmes's psychological interests are closely circumscribed by traditional fictive psychology,[8] has a mental structure consisting of "well-spread [moral] bases to [his head] for the ground-floor of the faculties, and well-vaulted arches for the upper range of apprehensions and combinations." [9] The minds of all three characters—Nora, Kitty, and Lindsay—are thoroughly enclosed and structurally rigid, and can accommodate only certain kinds of ideas in certain quantities and forms. In the passage from *Roderick Hudson,* however, mental structure is elastic and expands naturally under the pressure of constantly flowing and accumulating "material of thought." Ideas, like Irish immigrants, inevitably find or establish "relations" among their predecessors; somehow there is always room for one more.

In his reply associating mental pliancy with youth, and thus suggesting a basic link between psychology and physiology, Rowland alters the image of the room somewhat. "Open doors" replace elastic walls as the condition allowing for psychological movement or flow, and in Rowland's view this condition is the "best part" of experience. We might say that in James's view it offers the best angle from which to approach the problem of representing experience in fiction, or at least one of the most interesting aspects of that problem. Age will eventually close mental doors and erect a mental wall against which consciousness will "resound" without being able to move through it to "something beyond." The reverberating moment of consciousness, itself only momentarily basic to psychological representation in *Watch and Ward,* is no longer sufficient for James. At this point in *Roderick,* and at this stage of development in his fictive psychology, his main interest is in the movement of consciousness, and in the possibility of establishing, on the basis of such movement, a relation between psychic reverberation and the thrust of narrative toward "something beyond." It is this new sense of organic mental change, and its possible relation to the observation of organically developing experience in a fictive world, that James claims to have made intrinsically interesting, indeed "quite the stuff of [his] thesis" in *Roderick Hudson.*

Roderick's original question in the passage, "what becomes of all . . . the material of thought," contains another question, one bearing on the relation between James's emerging psychological concerns and his developing narrative method. Implied in the notion that "the more the mind takes in, the more it has space for," is the possibility that as the novelist focuses more intensely on mental processes, such processes ramify and expand to occupy more narrative space. The material of thought might itself become the basic material of fiction, and the flow of consciousness might be closely identified with the flow of narrative. This "curious" (or "strange") possibility is at the heart of James's effort to locate the "centre, the point of command of all the rest" in *Roderick Hudson,* in Rowland's mind. However, to the extent that the preface implies, he neither formulates the idea as a coherent theory in this work, nor implements it as a deliberate technique.

James's failure to do this is perhaps best explained by a final reference to the preface, specifically his statement that it is not simply the movement of Rowland's mind which is fundamentally interesting and important, but "rather, strictly, its movement in the particular connexion." Because, in other words, "the drama is the very drama of [a character's] consciousness," the novelist must do more than conceive theoretically of such a consciousness as being capable of focusing the situations and events of the novel for the reader. He must also dramatize the conception, dramatize his character's mind in time and space, dramatize its engagement with and responses to the shifting particulars of situation and circumstance. The dramatization of psychological particulars—the actual movement of the mind "in the particular connexion" as distinct from mental dynamics more abstractly and theoretically considered—is precisely what is generally lacking in *Roderick Hudson.* It is also what we shall see James developing as a key element of narrative in *The Portrait of a Lady,* and what we shall see him establish as the consistently dominant one in *The Ambassadors.*

The passage we have been discussing, for all its interest regarding change in the author's psychological assumptions, is a theoretical speculation about the nature of mental process, rather than a rendering of a specific mental sequence in the mind of either Roderick or Rowland. In this it is characteristic of the entire work. Despite James's reliance on third-person narration, Rowland's consciousness seems capable in a general way of "commanding" the events of the novel from his position in the psychological "centre." Yet James retains decided control over the novel's version of reality, and Rowland's perceptions of this reality tend to dissolve into James's without being fully exposed to or defined by the specific impressions which supposedly provoke them, or the "particular" circumstances in which they presumably occur. Rowland's mind remains essentially unaffected by what James calls in *The Ambassadors* the "common and constant pressure" of circumstance, in spite of his own theoretical interest in the psychological impact of a changed environment on Roderick and himself. The actual movements of his consciousness are diluted by abstraction and by frequent blending into the solution of James's presence as an author.

A brief illustration will suffice here. As the young sculptor and his benefactor feel their "roots striking and spreading in the Roman soil," Rowland grows increasingly uneasy about the "secret fund of strange alacrities" he has been hoarding in favor of Mary Garland, Roderick's fiancée back in Northampton. His unease proceeds as much from conscientious concern with the conventional obligations involved—his own toward Roderick and Roderick's toward Mary—as from a more deeply germinating awareness that he is himself in love with her. Sensing that Roderick, exhilarated at "just beginning to live into [his] possibilities," has lost interest in the girl, while she remains "as living a presence" to him as when he first met her, Rowland

> . . . had wondered over the whole matter first and last in a great many different ways—he had looked at it in all possible lights. There was something that mocked any sense of due sequences in the fact of [Roderick's] having fallen in love with [Mary]. She was not, as Rowland conceived her, the "type" that, other things being what they were, would most have touched him, and the mystery of attraction and desire, always so baffling if seen only from without, quite defied analysis here.[10]

The actual process of Rowland's "wondering," including the particular changes in the aspect of the mental gem produced by angling it "in all possible lights," is theoretically quite important: it leads to the conclusion, appearing somewhat later in the passage, that "any other girl would have answered Roderick's sentimental needs" at the time of his engagement to Mary. (That this conclusion is correct is less immediately interesting to James than the fact that it is in Rowland's interest to convince himself of its truth.) We are simply told, retrospectively and without elaboration, that such a process occurred, and that it "mocked" Rowland's preconceptions without really altering them or his sense of what might be "duly" expected to follow from them. We already know that Rowland tends to perceive people as types, but we do not learn anything specific about his conception of Mary's " 'type' " in connection with this particular problem. Nor do we find out what conditions the phrase "other things being what they were" is meant to comprehend. A complex relation between two characters, about which we are supposed to rely for information on the thoughts of a third, has been abstracted into "the mystery of attraction and desire," which even our observing intelligence can see "only from without" and which consequently "defies" his power of specific analysis.

Some solution to the mystery is important to the continuation of narrative, and James, his perceiver "baffled" along with his own capacity to dramatize the perceiver's mind directly, edges toward center stage. As the passage continues, we find a more detailed account of Rowland's thoughts, one which has in a sense been previously recorded by the novelist and is only now released into the narrative, with interpretive commentary. James tells us that Rowland *"would have been* [italics mine] at a loss to say" why Mary's type appealed to Roderick, had he really confronted the question. He notes that "our virtuous hero did scanty justice" to the idea that Roderick could hardly be held responsible for Rowland's "irregular" attraction to his betrothed. He makes sure we see the "subtle sophistry" of Rowland's mental argument that while "the charm for Roderick had been the circumstance of sex, the accident of nearness, the influence of youth," the charm for him was *"the* charm!—was the mysterious, individual, essential woman." Thus by the time we arrive at the concluding assertion, that Rowland "drifted, under these deep discretions indeed, nearer and nearer to the conviction that at just that crisis any other girl would have answered," we feel screened off from the character's mind. The psychological narrative lacks dramatic immediacy even though the notion of "drift" is quite in accord with the theory of organically flowing consciousness that distinguishes this novel from *Watch and Ward.*

As for Roderick, the same passage suggests that the inaccessibility of his interior processes runs throughout the work which bears his name. As a type of the romantic genius, indeed, he is almost literally without mental mechanics: in an earlier scene Rowland "went off envying [and not altogether ironically] the intellectual comfort of genius, which can arrive at serene conclusions without disagreeable processes." James endows Roderick less with a working mind than with a generalized temperament, to which Rowland and Roderick as well as James refer but which none of the three really explores. Roderick, like Rowland, talks a great deal about how impressions operate on perception. But Roderick's subjection to "the clutch of his temperament," like Rowland's to abstract rationality, relieves James of the technical need to portray—perhaps even prevents him from portraying—such operations, while in some sense accounting for their theoretical existence. Ultimately, the reader, along with Rowland and James, can view Roderick's actions "only from without."

Thus the conceptions underlying the fictive psychology of *Roderick Hudson* "remain happier than [their] execution," as James remarks in the preface. The psychological details of Roderick's disintegration as an artist and as a moral entity, theoretically "a gradual process, and of which the exhibitional interest is exactly that it *is* gradual and occasional, and thereby traceable and watchable," are omitted or obscured, just as we have seen Rowland's supposedly controlling perceptions diluted or obscured. There are, however, moments in the narrative at which concrete images seem to dramatize particular psychic events perfectly. At one point, for example, Rowland searches inwardly for the "afterglow of [a] frightened flash" of insight, a telling modification of the simpler flash of Nora Lambert's mental "spark." In another scene James creates a vivid sense of both the complex association and the fluid interpenetration of ideas in Rowland's mind:

> For forty-eight hours there swam before [his] eyes a vision of a wondrous youth, graceful and beautiful as he passed, plunging like a diver into a misty gulf. . . . Beyond this vision there faintly glimmered another, as in the children's game of the magic lantern a picture is superposed on the white wall before the last one has quite faded. It represented Mary Garland . . .[11]

There are several such moments, but they are isolated glimpses into, rather than sustained portrayals from within, the intricacies of a character's consciousness. But in *The Portrait of a Lady,* James's next large-scale novel, we find him extending his artistic control over the psychological theories broached in *Roderick Hudson,* and beginning to forge from these fragmentary glimpses a direct and continuous dramatization of the mind.

The celebrated forty-second chapter of *The Portrait of a Lady,* in which Isabel Archer Osmond keeps what James calls in his preface "my young woman's extraordinary meditative vigil," is, on at least two counts, the most interesting and relevant portion of the novel for our purposes. In the first place, James is concerned here with projecting the "view from within" his heroine's mind, at a pivotal point in her experience. Events are entirely internal—from the first sentence to the last, Isabel is alone, silent, and virtually motionless, although "in a fever" of mental activity. The movement of Isabel's consciousness, as it plays over the origins and implications of her involvement with Gilbert Osmond and Madame Merle, is the medium through which James attempts to portray a key phase in her encounter with the abrasive realities of her world. This chapter provides a strong test of the novelist's ability to dramatize a character's mind at length and "in the particular connexion," and reveals his progress toward solutions to the problems in the fictive psychology of *Roderick Hudson.*

Secondly, James's remarks in the preface about this section present us with an opportunity to observe, as we did in *Roderick Hudson,* the relation between current practice and retrospective theory in his fictive psychology. This opportunity is of course subject to the same limitations noted in connection with the earlier work: while the *Portrait* was serialized during 1880–81 and first issued in book form late in 1881, its preface was written for the publication of the 1908 New York Edition. Precisely because

James composed the prefaces to *Roderick* and *Portrait* at essentially the same time, however, and because both essays reflect essentially the same commitment to psychological representation as a principle of narrative continuity, they help us understand the nature and plot the rate of progress in the *Portrait* toward fulfillment of that commitment.

Two passages in particular from the "Preface to *The Portrait of a Lady*" seem to reiterate ideas first expressed in the preface to *Roderick*. Both are briefer and crisper than their more elaborately explicated prototypes (see pp. 43–44), as if to show that in the art of self-criticism as well as in the art of fiction James was developing conciseness and concreteness as he moved from the formulation toward the application of theory. Recalling his germinal idea for the story—"the mere slim shade of an intelligent but presumptuous girl" who was to be shown "affronting her destiny" —James goes on to discuss the "process of logical accretion" by which this wraith of a heroine was to be invested with the substance of a legitimate subject. This process is one of emerging relations, of the organic growth in the novelist's imagination of "the complications [she] would be most likely to produce and to feel." Such complications produce the overall "difficulty" of representation which James places highest among the "high attributes of a Subject." He writes:

> "Place the centre of the subject in the young woman's own consciousness," I said to myself, "and you get as interesting and as beautiful a difficulty as you could wish. Stick to *that*—for the centre; put the heaviest weight into *that* scale, which will be so largely the scale of her relation to herself." [12]

Thus James's answer to his own primary question—"What will she *do?*"—is that what Isabel "does" will bear narrative weight and approach the "centre" of the novel only through the medium of what she inwardly sees and feels:

> Without her sense of [her adventures], her sense *for* them, as one may say, they are next to nothing at all; but isn't the beauty and the difficulty just in showing their mystic conversion by that sense, conversion into the stuff of drama? . . .[13]

The shift from an idea of interior process as "the stuff of one's thesis" in *Roderick Hudson* to a notion of such process as "the stuff of drama" in *The Portrait of a Lady* is perhaps slight, though highly interesting in view of our concern with movement from the abstractly theoretical toward the concretely dramatized in psychological representation. This verbal shift acquires significance as James turns to what he considers his most "consistent application of that ideal"—Isabel's vigil in Chapter 42. In the preface he writes:

> Reduced to its essence, it is but the vigil of searching criticism; but it throws the action further forward than twenty "incidents" might have done. It was designed to have all the vivacity of incident and all the economy of picture. She sits up, by her dying fire, far into the night, under the spell of recognitions on which she finds the last sharpness suddenly wait. It is a representation simply of her motionless *seeing,* and an attempt to make the still lucidity of her act as "interesting" as the surprise of a caravan or the identification of a pirate. It represents, for that matter, one of the identifications dear to the novelist, and even indispensable to him; but it all goes on without her being approached by another person and without her leaving her chair. It is obviously the best thing in the book, but it is only a supreme illustration of the general plan.[14]

A judgment as to the actual consistency of the "illustration" with the "ideal" must await our own analysis of James's fictive psychology in this sequence of the novel. Nevertheless, it already seems clear that a "general plan" of narrative development in which the contents of consciousness generate thrust and concentrate interest is gaining force and cohesion in James's work.

Isabel Archer, young, beautiful, naïve though intelligent—in short "the heiress of all the ages" setting out to claim her inheritance—goes from Albany to England with Mrs. Touchett, her aunt, and has a fortune settled on her by her dying uncle, an expatriated American banker. The bequest is arranged secretly by her consumptive cousin Ralph Touchett, who is in love with Isabel without hope of success because of his health. He hopes instead, by making her independent, to ensure for her a "high destiny," and for himself a vicarious share in a life he envisions as "soaring far up in the blue— . . . sailing in the bright light." Having refused an offer of marriage from the Touchett's titled and wealthy neighbor Lord Warburton, and turned aside the persistent American ardor of Caspar Goodwood, who has followed her to Europe, Isabel takes her vague ideals of freedom and fulfilling experience to Florence. There Serena Merle, an accomplished and somewhat mysterious woman of forty, American by birth but European by experience, introduces her to Gilbert Osmond, American expatriate and a fortune-hunting esthete, to whose cultivated taste and apparent nobility of mind Isabel is drawn. Unaware that Osmond and Madame Merle were once lovers and that Madame Merle is the mother of his daughter Pansy (ostensibly the child of an earlier marriage), Isabel marries him in spite of protest from Ralph, who accurately detects the arid narrowness of Osmond's nature and who sees in the match an end to his dream for Isabel's future. During the months that follow, she gradually senses Osmond's lack of interest in her, indeed feels his contempt for her as anything other than a well-chosen and well-displayed *objet d'art.* She struggles to vindicate her judgment by trying to please her husband, but as the marriage continues to deteriorate she turns her attention increasingly to Pansy and resolves—with a certain sense of her own heroism—to transcend her mistake by "just immensely (oh, with the highest grandeur!)" accepting it.

At this point "an accumulation of inflammable material" is ignited in Isabel's mind and the extended psychological sequence with which we are concerned is precipitated. Osmond and Madame Merle, separately, but in such a way that Isabel dimly discerns the possibility of an obscure relation, suggest that she use her influence over her former suitor Warburton to secure his marriage to Pansy. Their suggestions seem subtly like commands, or the requests of those in a position of manipulative power, and without in the least understanding the rising "confusion of regrets, [the] complication of fears" within her, Isabel begins to reflect on her sense of entanglement.

James simultaneously crystallizes this sense in, and launches the longer process of reflection with, an image of her uncomprehending perception into the deep design of Osmond's relation to Serena Merle. Coming upon them in the drawing-room, their conversation having lapsed for a moment into a "familiar silence," Isabel notes that Osmond is sitting while Madame Merle stands and that they seem to be "musing, face to face, with the freedom of old friends who sometimes exchange ideas without uttering them":

> There was nothing to shock in this; they were old friends in fact. But the thing made an image, lasting only a moment, like a sudden flicker of light. Their relative positions, their absorbed mutual gaze, struck her as something detected. But it was all over by the time she had fairly seen it.[15]

Shortly afterward, Osmond having made his suggestion to her regarding Warburton and Pansy, Isabel becomes "absorbed in looking at," if not immediately able to "fairly see" or clearly interpret, the flow of ideas generated by the sudden flicker of this mental flame:

> She had answered nothing because his words had put the situation before her and she was absorbed in looking at it.

There was something in them that suddenly made vibrations deep, so that she had been afraid to trust herself to speak. After he had gone she leaned back in her chair and closed her eyes; and for a long time, far into the night and still further, she sat in the still drawing-room, given up to her meditation. . . . Osmond had told her to think of what he had said; and she did so indeed, and of many other things. The suggestion from another that she had a definite influence on Lord Warburton—this had given her the start that accompanies unexpected recognition. Was it true that there was something still between them that might be a handle to make him declare himself to Pansy? . . . Isabel had hitherto not asked herself the question, because she had not been forced; but now that it was directly presented to her she saw the answer, and the answer frightened her. Yes, there was something—something on Lord Warburton's part. . . . It was as thin as a hair, but there were moments when she seemed to hear it vibrate. For herself nothing was changed. . . . But he? Had he still the idea that she might be more to him than other women? Had he the wish to profit by the memory of the few moments of intimacy through which they had once passed? . . . What were his hopes, his pretensions, and in what strange way were they mingled with his evidently very sincere appreciation of poor Pansy? . . . Was she to cultivate the advantage she possessed in order to make him commit himself to Pansy, knowing that he would do so for her sake and not for the small creature's own—was this the service her husband asked of her? . . . Isabel wandered among these ugly possibilities until she had completely lost her way. . . . Then she broke out of the labyrinth, rubbing her eyes, and declared that her imagination surely did her little honour and that her husband's did him even less. Lord Warburton was as disinterested as he need be, and she was no more to him than she need wish. She would rest upon this till the contrary should be proved; proved more effectually than by a cynical intimation of Osmond's.[16]

The opening lines of this passage suggest at first glance a set of psychological assumptions more archaic than advanced. Osmond has presented Isabel with the fictive "situation" (in its simplest sense), saying that he counts upon her to arrange matters between Pansy and Warburton, and Isabel is looking *at* this situation, seemingly as a discrete and uncomplicated moral problem. The question of Osmond's right, or her own, to determine Pansy's fate, whether or not for the sake of adding Warburton's peerage to Osmond's collection of *objets,* has entered the story and appears at the outset to be the focus of narrative interest. Insofar as Isabel's more specifically psychological engagement with the problem seems relevant, the setting creates a sense of classically circumscribed introspection: she is sitting alone with her thoughts in the quiet darkness of a room recalling the "close-curtained" contemplative retreats from the action of the earlier novels. The word "meditation" suggests rational control over mental experience having an assumed relation to moral considerations, and James apparently plans to describe this experience through an omniscient third person.

The words "vibrations deep" in the second sentence, however, appear in a context suggesting other possibilities. In the early editions this sentence begins: "There was something in them that suddenly opened the door to agitation. . . ." "Agitation" is itself a blanket term for a wide range of mental states, but while the image contains the sense of static, generalized excitement, it also contains the possibility of more particularized psychological motion. Agitation might be a mental intruder, "floated [through the door] into [Isabel's] mind by the current of life," as James speculates in the preface. Or, it might be something she experiences during a mental journey, not necessarily voluntary, through the suddenly opened door, down a hall, or into a series of rooms. James's "door" dictates my extension into "hall" or "rooms," but this is an example of the effect a particular word can have on the development of an idea requiring different vocabulary. What James is attempting to dramatize is an idea of consciousness not as a series of separated or "walled" states, but as continuous flow encompassing states which exist individually only through their mutual relations. His revision—"There was something in them that suddenly made vibrations deep"—does not in itself effect such a dramatization. It does, however, free his conception of a reverberating moment in the character's mind from restraining rigidity, and enable these vibrations to spread through the passage as it unfolds. The vagueness with which Isabel apprehends the "something" which first "opened the door to agitation" and eventually "made vibrations deep," moreover, hints at the existence of indistinct eddies along the peripheries of such a stream, penumbral zones of semiconscious if not wholly unconscious awareness.

This is of course placing a heavy burden on a single sentence, but as the passage continues the burden is shared. James's report that Isabel pondered what Osmond had said along with "many other things" comes altogether from without his heroine's mind, but the "start that accompanies unexpected recognition" brings us closer to a focus on the inner workings of that mind. As in the case of the opening door, the shift may be viewed in terms of a single word: "start." At the simplest level, James clearly means "jolt" or sudden "surprise," with "recognition" following as a relatively simple perception proceeding from a simple source, Osmond's "suggestion." Yet James now spends an entire page exploring and bringing to completion in Isabel's mind this particular psychic event. He thus endows "start" with the sense of "beginning," the setting in motion of a complex process of recognition which may end, like a stream, a great distance from its source.

At this point James's attention shifts further away from exposition and closer to direct examination of this process of recognition. The basic answer to Isabel's introspective question—"Yes, there was something" between Warburton and herself—appears early in the sequence, and in conventional terms would be sufficient psychological anchorage for a continuing narrative of external events.

Like her mental "start," however, Isabel's answer releases narrative energy of its own—it "vibrates," further intensifying and bringing toward the dramatic surface the "vibrations deep" within her at the outset of the passage. Rather than concentrating on the importance to external plot of Warburton's feeling toward her, James focuses on the internal reverberations generated by her discovery of that feeling, and on the impetus they provide to her gathering effort to fathom her situation.

Through most of the remainder of the passage these accumulating reverberations take the form of accumulating mental questions, posed from within Isabel's consciousness and, although still cast in the third person, divested of most authorial trappings. (James is never very far off, however; his diction continues to dominate, and phrases such as "Isabel had hitherto not asked herself" occasionally intrude.) The questions pile up in irregular cadences, suggesting not methodically rational analysis but the impulsive, unevenly shifting currents of a mind picking its way over unfamiliar, even hostile and "frightening" interior terrain.

And indeed, when Isabel breaks "out of the labyrinth," having wandered and lost her way in such terrain, she makes only a momentary—and illusory—escape. That "Lord Warburton was as disinterested as he need be, and she was no more to him than she need wish" shows that her conscious determinations need not accord with objective reality. Something nearer the truth lies somewhere in the labyrinthine turnings of her thought.

At the beginning of *Roderick Hudson,* Rowland "engaged to believe that all women were fair, all men were brave and the world a delightful place of sojourn, until the contrary should be distinctly proved." In theory, but not in dramatically represented fact, the "friction of existence" taught him his error. Isabel's resolution here to "rest upon [her idea of Warburton's disinterestedness] till the contrary should be proved" might stand for all of her faulty assumptions about the nature of reality, assumptions which the novel is centrally concerned to test. As her interior wandering continues beyond this passage, James concentrates more insistently on showing—molding into the very "stuff of [his] drama"—the psychological processes through which the frictions of Isabel's existence erode her illusions and refine her awareness:

> Such a resolution, however, brought her this evening but little peace, for her soul was haunted with terrors which crowded to the foreground of thought as quickly as a place was made for them. What had suddely set them into livelier motion she hardly knew, unless it were the strange impression she had received in the afternoon of her husband's being in more direct communication with Madame Merle than she suspected. This impression came back to her from time to time, and now she wondered that it had never come before. Besides this, her short interview with Osmond half an hour ago was a striking example of his faculty for making everything wither that he touched, spoiling everything for her that he looked at. . . . Was the fault in himself, or only in the deep mistrust she had conceived for him? This mistrust was the clearest result of their short married life; a gulf had opened between them over which they looked at each other with eyes that were on either side a declaration of the deception suffered. . . . It was not her fault—she had practised no deception; she had only admired and believed. She had taken all the first steps in the purest confidence, and then she had suddenly found the infinite vista of a multiplied life to be a dark, narrow alley with a dead wall at the end. . . . It was her deep distrust of her husband—this was what darkened the world. That is a sentiment easily indicated, but not so easily explained, and so composite in its character that much time and still more suffering had been needed to bring it to its actual perfection. Suffering, with Isabel, was an active condition; it was not a chill, a stupor, a despair; it was a passion of thought, of speculation, of response to every pressure. . . . It had come gradually—it was not till the first year of their life together, so admirably intimate at first, had closed that she had taken the alarm. Then the shadows had begun

> to gather; it was as if Osmond deliberately, almost malignantly, had put the lights out one by one. The dusk at first was vague and thin, and she could still see her way in it. But it steadily deepened. . . . There were times when she almost pitied him; for if she had not deceived him in intention she understood how completely she must have done so in fact. She had effaced herself when he first knew her; she had made herself small, pretending there was less of her than there really was . . . He was not changed; he had not disguised himself . . . any more than she. But she had seen only half his nature then, as one saw the disk of the moon when it was partly masked by the shadow of the earth. She saw the full moon now—she saw the whole man.[17]

In his chapter on "The Stream of Consciousness" in *Principles of Psychology* (1890), William James states that each "image in the mind is steeped and dyed in the free water [of consciousness] that flows round it. With it goes the sense of its relations, near and remote, the dying echo of whence it came to us, the dawning sense of whither it is to lead. The significance, the value, of the image is all in this halo or penumbra that surrounds and escorts it."[18] Henry James's interest in Isabel's fading but recurrently echoing image of Osmond and Madame Merle in the drawing-room, and in her dawning sense of the meanings toward which this "strange impression" is directing her thought, is similar. For the novelist, the dramatic significance and narrative value of the image is also largely a matter of the penumbral associations through which it is steeped and dyed in the total volume of Isabel's conscious flow.

Driven by the continuous pressure of that flow, and set into still livelier motion by the vibrations of her recurring impression, inchoate "terrors" move involuntarily from the clouded periphery of Isabel's mental stream toward the clearer and deeper "foreground of thought" in its central current. Within the general notion of stream, however, the connotations of James's language describing their movement are somewhat confusedly complex. On the one hand, these unformed ideas "crowd" into closer and more cohesive relations, taking on definite shape and gathering narrative mass as they become concentrated in the foreground of thought. They generate dramatic thrust in the same sense that a compressed mass generates heat. On the other hand, the same ideas accumulate and expand in Isabel's mind to occupy space "as quickly as a place was made for them," actually making room for themselves by displacing others from the mental pool or by raising its level and extending its boundaries. In either case James's conception of this process offsets the archaic ring of the omniscient phrase "her soul was haunted." In both cases, the material of Isabel's thought is advancing to the foreground of James's dramatic interest, becoming the substance with which he will attempt to supply certain crucial shadings to her portrait as the passage and the chapter proceed.

One such shading—and the central psychological event of the passage—is the shift in her mind from the conviction that the gulf between Osmond and herself "was not her fault—she had practised no deception," to an understanding of "how completely she must have done so in fact" if not in intention. The thematic consequences of this interior change are considerable. James is less concerned with rendering a simple judgment against Osmond for the sense of mutual distrust and deception which has poisoned the marriage, than with bringing Isabel to a nascent awareness of her own capacity for self-deception. Her view of the "full moon," Osmond's sterile nature unobscured by either the mist of his calculated charm or the "shadow" of her charmed miscalculation of him, is, partly, an amplified view of herself, and reveals how her own limited vision has contributed to the present situation. In broader terms, this part of the passage brings into full view—for Isabel and the reader—the conflict between her earlier ideal of a life devoted to soaring among the "high places of happiness," and her present sense of a harsh reality forcing her "downward and earthward, into realms of restriction and depression." What the novel offers by way of resolution for such conflict lies mainly in the area of heightened awareness, of experience psychologically absorbed, rather than in the area of literal incident. Thus, the novelist's close attention to a process leading toward enhanced awareness, one which retrospectively focuses and registers the meaning of Isabel's experience, indeed "throws the action further forward than twenty 'incidents' might have done," as James says in his preface. At any rate, it throws the action forward in a manner and for a purpose that attention to external incident, rather than to the view from within, would not permit.

James's record of this mental shift also suggests a relation between change in his fictive psychology and change in his idea of the heroine's role in fiction. Like the innocents of *Watch and Ward* and *A Chance Acquaintance,* Isabel "had only admired and believed" in Osmond without perceiving his complexity, "had taken all the first steps in the purest confidence." "Pure" confidence is precisely the quality that sees Nora Lambert and Kitty Ellison through—in each case the heroine's unassailable innocence eventually resolves conflict and brings the conditions of reality into line with the abstract values she represents. The "hideous alteration" of Nora's world by her discovery of Lawrence's plan to marry her is actually superficial and temporary. Here in the *Portrait,* however, the heroine's innocence is a more complicated and ambiguous quality, a source of vulnerability instead of control. Isabel is in the process of discovering a reality which forcibly imposes its conditions on her abstract assumptions. The change in her life wrought by her marriage to Osmond is deep and lasting. Thus by setting her "purest" innocence irretrievably in the fictive past at this point, James seems also to leave behind the notion of such innocence as a primary basis for characterization. The psychological shock waves resulting from the collision of innocence with reality are now his real subject; he is less interested in the "first steps" than in the mental sequence linking those that follow.

James had an opportunity in *Roderick Hudson* to pursue this by developing such a sequence. Mary Garland, like Isabel, is a heroine whose "purity and rigidity of . . . mind" are exposed to the corroding effects of experience in a world far more dangerously complex than she imagines it to be. Corrosion does indeed occur—Roderick's destruction and Mary's disillusionment are ultimately complete. Yet James, whose characterizations in this work are conventionally polarized despite his theoretical interests in psychic complexity (Mary the fair innocent, Christina the dark temptress; reasonable Rowland, temperamental Roderick), does not really conceive of Mary as having traceable interior reactions to experience. Instead, she is permanently stunned by her collision with reality; her suffering, unlike Isabel's, *is* a passive, static, generalized condition, "a chill, a stupor, a despair." Because her inward life remains frozen rather than being set in livelier motion by the pressure of experience, Mary fades from the dramatic center of the novel and her narrative potential remains unrealized.

Isabel's inward life constitutes the dramatic center at this point in the *Portrait,* and the narrative itself consists in her mental responsiveness "to every pressure." Both her "deep distrust" of Osmond—James's most immediate representational problem—and the more general suffering from which it proceeds belong to an "active," organically "composite" psychological condition. James is thematically concerned with bringing this condition "to its actual perfection" in Isabel's mind. He is technically concerned with representing the process of its perfection or completion on the printed page, and he requires not only "much [fictive] time" but also considerable narrative space to do so. He sees Isabel's mind as existing and operating in time and space, as subject to impression and circumstance, despite her passion for abstract "speculation" and notwithstanding that the whole sequence "goes on without her being approached by another person and without her leaving her chair," as he says in the preface. Whereas in *Roderick Hudson* characters tend to withdraw from the action to speculate on the operations of their own minds, here the action itself occurs *in* a speculative process of a character's mind, a process which is activated by a specific impression created by a particular set of circumstances.

The composite complexity and gradual, organic nature of this process counter the archaic effect of James's confession that it is something "easily indicated, but not so easily explained." Indeed, even if James were more completely concerned than he is here with omnisciently explaining rather than with representing Isabel's thought, his evident concern with analyzing its content instead of unanalytically "indicating" its presence would be significant. As it is, the novelist's scrutiny of his heroine's mind blends smoothly with the movements of her own self-scrutiny through most of the passage. Intrusions such as "Isabel had hitherto not asked herself" are now virtually absent, and third-person intrusions approximate convincingly, though they fail to reproduce exactly, the links in her own train of thought. Only in the notions of Isabel's distrust as a force capable of "darkening the world," or of her mounting sense of oppression as "gathering shadows" or "deepening dusk," or of her incomplete view of Osmond as the "disk of the moon . . . partly masked," does James strike an archaic note. On these occasions his language and imagery, while by no means ineffective, suggest earlier reflections of conventionally simplified inner states in passages of natural description.

Within this frame, then, Isabel arrives at the understanding toward which the "start [of] unexpected recognition" propelled her at the beginning of the chapter, and James simultaneously moves closer to "one of the identifications dear to the novelist." Neither her enlarged awareness of the sources of her situation, however, nor James's intimation to the reader of Osmond's true relation to Madame Merle, is brought to completion in the passage or even in the chapter. Isabel's vigil continues, the narrative of her mind shifting and focusing according to her own strengths and weaknesses of insight, breaking momentarily out of the labyrinth only to resume the exploration of its recesses. The chapter ends as it began, with Isabel absorbed in and baffled by the recurring "vision . . . of her husband and Madame Merle unconsciously and familiarly associated." Yet, she has gained in moral understanding if not in factual knowledge, and James has enriched if not yet completed her portrait. Both these advances in dramatic intensity result from placing the narrative "centre" in the interior setting of her consciousness, and from extended narrative attention to the mental fever which rises as the fire by which she sits in the exterior setting smolders and dies.

Nevertheless, this section of the novel is but a "supreme illustration of the general plan" which James leaves unimplemented or implements unevenly elsewhere in the work. Nowhere else in the *Portrait* does he project the view from within at such length or with such care for the movement of consciousness "in the particular connexion." Because of this, the vigil chapter itself remains something of a tour de force, a centerpiece dominating but not integrating the whole. James claims in his preface to have shown in this chapter "what an exciting inward life may do for the person leading it even while it remains perfectly normal." Yet Isabel's inward life in the sequence, "feverish," "assailed by visions," "in a state of extraordinary activity," scarcely strikes us as perfectly normal, whatever it shows about James's progress in converting such life into the stuff of drama. In *The Ambassadors,* however, which he considered "quite the best, 'all round,' of my productions," James makes good his claim, and through his portrayal of the inward life of Lambert Strether brings his general plan of psychological representation to full dramatic life.

Writing in 1909, much closer in time to his composition of *The Ambassadors* (1903) than the prefaces to *Roderick Hudson* and *The Portrait of a Lady* stand in relation to those works, James begins his preface to this novel with an untypically direct and positive assertion: "Nothing is more easy than to state the subject of *The Ambassadors.*" Nothing had seemed more difficult, or at any rate more complicated, for James in the two earlier essays than to "state"—rather than gradually to encircle in abstract prose—the subject of *Roderick* or of the *Portrait,* especially regarding the place of dramatized consciousness among the "high attributes of a Subject." Here, however, the novelist points immediately to a specific passage, "planted or 'sunk,' stiffly and saliently, in the centre of the current," as containing not only the thematic essence of the story but also the key to its narrative momentum and representational design. The passage in question is Strether's speech to little Bilham in Gloriani's garden, in which he laments his mistake in not really having "had" his life, and which he concludes with the famous exhortation to "Live!" Of this passage James writes:

> He [Strether] has accordingly missed too much, though perhaps after all constitutionally qualified for a better part, and he wakes up to it in conditions that press the spring of a terrible question. *Would* there yet perhaps be time for reparation?—reparation, that is, for the injury done his character? . . . The answer to which is that he now at all events *sees;* so that the business of my tale and the march of my action, not to say the precious moral of everything, is just my demonstration of this process of vision.[19]

James thus explicitly equates the "march" of fictive action with the movement of a fictive mind, and defines his primary artistic business as the continuous portrayal of such movement. In his preface to *The Portrait of a Lady,* he described Isabel's vigil as a "representation simply of her motionless *seeing,* and an attempt withal to make the still lucidity of her act . . . 'interesting.' " Even in retrospect of a finished work, his language suggests a limited experiment producing not-quite-certain results, one requiring the subject to be immobilized and isolated in order for her mental life to be brought into sharp focus and set into livelier motion. Here, however, James imposes no such restrictions. The current of dramatic action into which he so saliently sinks the scene in Gloriani's garden is also the current of Strether's mind, and it flows the length of the novel. Strether *"sees"* throughout, clearly or distortedly as the case may be, and whether or not he is alone or in repose. James is concerned to have the reader observe this process of vision from within. He entrusts the "precious moral of everything," moreover, to his concern with psychological representation, saying in the preface that "the point is not in the least what to make of [the story], but only . . . to put one's hand on" a story which "simply makes for itself." From the prescribed moral assumptions of *Watch and Ward,* which in the terms of that work authenticate or certify as "real" the subordination of mental process to abstract values, he has arrived at a commitment in *The Ambassadors* to "the authenticity of concrete experience," realizable only *through* close narrative attention to mental process.

Thus the process of Strether's vision is less an act of still lucidity, aimed like Isabel's at moral understanding, than an organic sequence of involuntary and sometimes violent *re*actions to concrete experience, many of which are morally disorienting. Thus, having succinctly stated his literary aims, James proceeds to elaborate:

> I accounted for everything . . . by the view that he [Strether] had come to Paris in some state of mind which was literally undergoing, as a result of new and unexpected assaults and infusions, a change almost from hour to hour. He had come with a view that might have been figured by a clear green liquid, say, in a neat glass phial; and the liquid, once poured into the open cup of *application,* once exposed to the action of another air, had begun to turn from green to red, or whatever, and might, for all he knew, be on its way to purple, to black, to yellow. . . . [He had] presented himself at the gate . . . primed with a moral scheme of the most approved pattern which was yet framed to break down on any approach to vivid facts . . .[20]

Here the novelist precisely "figures" a fully developed interest which was only implicit in his comments on the earlier novels, and only partially explored in them: his interest in the cumulative impact of circumstances on consciousness, in the transformation wrought on an abstract "scheme" by exposure to concrete "facts." In *Roderick Hudson,* the effects of the friction of existence on Rowland's mind are theoretically but not dramatically accounted for, while the shock of disillusionment stuns Mary, paralyzing her psychologically and precluding any detailed narrative account of her response. In *The Portrait of a Lady,* the pressure of reality sets up vibrations in Isabel's mind which reach a fever pitch of narrative intensity during her vigil, but which are only intermittently accounted for in dramatic detail elsewhere in the novel. In *The Ambassadors,* the unremitting infusion of immediate impressions into Strether's mind causes literal, basic, continuing change of an almost biochemical nature, through the steady observation of which James "accounts for everything" in the story, just as he locates the "moral of everything" squarely in his demonstration of the process.

The literalness of the change, the vividness of the facts which enforce it, the emphasis on the application of abstractions to experience, the specific elaboration of the chemical analogy—all confirm and extend the drift noted earlier toward greater concreteness of idea and metaphor in critical remarks relating to fictive psychology as well as in the actual portrayal of characters' minds. The "instant of time" which, as James intimates but does not demonstrate in *Watch and Ward,* may have narrative potential as an extended mental process if viewed from within, has become a novel-long succession of moments comprising such a process and viewed from within "almost from hour to hour." The closed moral system of *Watch and Ward* and the sheltered psychological speculations in *Roderick Hudson,* effectively paralleled here in the neatly corked vial of Strether's moral scheme, have become the "open cup" of direct experience in which theory must undergo the test of application to real conditions. An abstract idea of the friction of existence in *Roderick* and a partial dramatization of interior response to every pressure in the *Portrait* have become the carefully recorded "action of another air" on Strether's consciousness, action producing specific effects in traceable sequence. That such action should erode values "of the most approved pattern"—values which frame and restrict psychological representation in *Watch and Ward* but which are themselves expressly "framed to break down" here—crowns the development of a theory of fiction in which psychological representation "accounts for everything."

James's ideal in this case, then, is essentially the same as that set forth in the prefaces to *Roderick* (a "geometry" the key theorem in which is the movement of consciousness "in the particular connexion") and to the *Portrait* (the "mystic conversion" of such movement into "the stuff of drama"), though he states it here with more concrete certainty of aim and skill: "the projection of [Strether's] consciousness . . . from beginning to end without intermission or deviation." Other characters figure in the novelist's plan and require his attention; but, he says, "Strether's sense of these things, and Strether's only, should avail me for showing them." The correspondence between prefatory (albeit after the fact) theory and fictive practice in *The Ambassadors,* however, is substantially closer than in either of the other cases.

Consider, for example, the arrival of Gloriani, a secondary character in both *Roderick Hudson* and *The Ambassadors,* on the narrative stage in each work.[21] The occasion in *Roderick* is a dinner party given by Rowland shortly after he and Roderick arrive in Rome, at which Gloriani, an accomplished sculptor, is a guest. Before this scene, however, Gloriani enters the story through an introductory "daguerreotype" by James, removed from the action and complete with an omniscient sketch of his life, character, and esthetic views. James acknowledges in a very general way Rowland's allegedly controlling point of view—the passage summarizes Rowland's previous knowledge of Gloriani and indicates his present attitude toward him. But the introduction remains authorial, and Gloriani remains less a person directly present to Rowland's mind than an abstract type conceived in James's.

Gloriani enters *The Ambassadors,* however, by coming directly into Strether's angle of vision and slipping directly into the current of his consciousness. As a result, we know less about him initially than we do in *Roderick,* but we are able, along with Strether, to "see" a great deal more than Rowland does. The occasion again is a party, the gathering in Gloriani's garden to which Chad Newsome brings Strether, and later during which Strether delivers to little Bilham the speech James mentioned in the preface as having been "planted . . . in the centre" of the story's development. From the moment of Strether's arrival at Gloriani's home, James focuses on the interior effect of the immediately visual:

> The place itself was a great impression—a small pavilion, clear-faced and sequestered, an effect of polished parquet, of fine white panel and spare, sallow gilt. . . . Far back from streets and unsuspected by crowds, reached by a long passage and a quiet court, it was as striking to the unprepared mind, he immediately saw, as a treasure dug up; giving him too, more than anything yet, the note of the range of the immeasurable town, and sweeping away, as by a last brave brush, his usual landmarks and terms; . . . he had the sense of names in the air, of ghosts at the windows, of signs and tokens, a whole range of expression all about him, too thick for prompt discrimination.
>
> This assault of images became for a moment, in the address of the distinguished sculptor, almost formidable: Gloriani showed him, in such perfect confidence, on Chad's introduction of him, a fine worn handsome face, a face that was like an open letter in a foreign tongue. With his genius in his eyes, his manners on his lips, his long career behind him and his honours and rewards all round, the great artist in the course of a single sustained look and a few words of delight at receiving him, affected our friend as a dazzling

> prodigy of type. Strether had seen in museums . . . the work of his hand; knowing too that after an earlier time in his native Rome he had migrated, in mid-career, to Paris, where, with a personal lustre almost violent, he shone in a constellation: all of which was more than enough to crown him, for his guest, with the light, with the romance of glory. Strether, in contact with that element as he had never yet so intimately been, had the consciousness of opening to it, for the happy instant, all the windows of his mind, of letting this rather gray interior drink in for once the sun of a clime not marked in his old geography.[22]

Rome's influence on Roderick Hudson is huge yet abstract—the idea rather than the objects of antiquity, far less the mingled features of a city both ancient and contemporary, prompts his sense of being changed and his speculation on the inpouring material of thought—and James pays no attention at all to the physical setting of the dinner party with Gloriani. Here, by contrast, "the place itself was a great impression" made up of many small (and specifically noted) impressions and "effects"—of parquet, of panel, of gilt. Paris, like Rome, is an "immeasurable" idea as well as a city, a symbol, as James says in the preface, "of more things than had been dreamt of in the philosophy [or marked in the "geography"] of Woollett." Yet it becomes so for Strether because of, rather than instead of, particular "notes" which the immediate details of a particular Parisian setting "strike" on his unprepared mind. The "long passage and . . . quiet court" through which Strether approaches Gloriani's garden have symbolic overtones, as the statement in the preface, that he arrives "through winding [mental] passages, through alternations of darkness and light," at an expanded sense of the significance of Paris, points out. Their symbolic value, however (as well as a pun on the passage of text through which Strether's thought is winding), depends on their existence as firmly literal aspects of the physical situation. Precise perceptual "brush" strokes, climaxing the mental excavation of a treasure charged with unsuspected meanings, are required to "sweep away" the conventionally limited landmarks and terms of his previous view of the city. Such strokes lay the representational groundwork for an extension in the range of his experience, for the mapping of new contours in his "interior . . . geography," the process which is James's larger concern in the passage as well as in the novel.

Place thus becomes, through an "assault" of specific images and the vaguer mental "signs and tokens" released by removal of Strether's usual reference points, fused with what James refers to just before the passage begins as the total "medium of the scene." That medium is a heightened psychological sensitivity on Strether's part to a broadened "range of expression all about him," a quickened flow within his consciousness of the resulting impressions and associations. James effects Gloriani's entry into the story through Chad's introduction of him directly into the dramatic medium of Strether's mind. Whereas in *Roderick* we learn only (and at the very end of James's introductory "daguerreotype") that Gloriani *"might* have been [italics mine], facially, for firmness, one of his own expensive bronzes," Strether's first impression is of a face unequivocally showing certain specified qualities, a face whose expression of mingled frankness and mystery *was* to him like the more concretely imagined "open letter in a foreign tongue." Whereas Gloriani's "genius" is subject to lengthy evaluation by James in the earlier novel, Strether's sense of his genius springs from the sculptor's eyes, shaping itself just beyond the passage into an impression of those eyes as filled with "the penetrating radiance . . . of the illustrious spirit itself." Gloriani's "manners," noted in *Roderick* as being gracefully deferential, express themselves directly to Strether in a cordial word of welcome. The "honours and rewards" of a career which James summarizes in *Roderick* but which Strether simply sees as fulfilled, are concretely present to Strether's mind in the tasteful luxury of Gloriani's dwelling and the crowd of admiring guests. All these impressions, conveyed to Strether in a "single, sustained look" from his host, coalesce to produce his sense of the artist as a "dazzling prodigy of type."

Gloriani's "type" in *Roderick Hudson,* as James briefly outlines it, is the extravagantly talented, vividly opinionated, possibly depraved expatriate artist (he is an American of French extraction, "or remotely perhaps of Italian"). Here, however, whatever his traits in the absolute (he is now a "native" Italian, older and more leonine in bearing), the "dazzle" of his presence rather than the outline of his character affects Strether as prodigious. Gloriani has been to Strether, even before their meeting, the supreme type of the creative artist, and James interpolates only those details of his achievement and experience which have directly contributed to this notion: Strether's having seen Gloriani's work in museums and having known of his dominant position in the constellation of Parisian artists. Contact occurring within Strether's mind, between the abstract "element" of imagined glory and the concrete impressions packed into the moment of actual meeting, is what "dazzles," what leads to "the consciousness of opening . . . all the windows of his mind" to streams of brilliant sunlight.

At one point in *Roderick* James imagines Mary's mind as a "clear ample 'spare-room' " in a traditional New England house, "with its windows up for ventilation." Here, he shows Strether in the psychological act of opening *all* his mental windows, not for ventilation by familiar breezes or for prospects on familiar scenes, but for the stronger, less predictable "action of another air," to quote the preface. The "interior" of Strether's mental house, furnished in conventional style and dulled to "gray" by the intellectual weather of Woollett, is brightened and perhaps even changed —shown to harbor unsuspected colors and spaces—by his total impression of Gloriani and the Parisian "climate" of experience. His awareness of change lasts only a "happy instant"; yet from within that instant he senses the possibility that his old geography—moral, intellectual, psychological—is being subtly revised through processes engendered by the literal geographical shift from Woollett to Paris.

Strether has undertaken this journey on behalf of his fiancée Mrs. Newsome, a rigidly conventional widow whose son Chad, who has been living in Europe for several years, ignores her requests that he return to Massachusetts and assume responsibility of the family business. Strether has arrived in Paris to find Chad changed, seemingly made over into an "absolutely *new* quantity" by his European experience, a central feature of which is his relationship with the cultured and worldly Madame de Vionnet. Himself a widower of middle age, Strether has brought to Paris an outlook "of the most approved [New England] pattern," in light of which Chad's liaison seems morally dubious at best. But Strether has also brought a highly sensitive imagination and a habit of "intense reflexion" upon his own reactions to a new environment. Confronted in Chad with the end result of a process both baffling and fascinating, a process whose phases and nuances he was not present to observe, Strether now feels himself immersed in the "fathomless medium" through which the process occurred. The categories of Woollett tend to "melt away" in this medium, and as he grows accustomed to its shifting lights and altered perspectives he becomes progressively less concerned with his ambassadorial duty. His sense of a new geography, still largely unmapped but already as real to him as the old, increasingly absorbs him.

The medium of the scene in Gloriani's garden, then, holds the new Strether and the old in suspension, precariously balanced. This balance is upset by the bitterness at having begun to "see" so late that Strether expresses, shortly after having met Gloriani, to little Bilham. The "reservoir" of his mind "filled sooner than he knew" by impressions of a world wider, indeed other than his own, he is overwhelmed by the overflow and "long, slow rush" to full consciousness of their collective meaning for him:

> Live all you can; it's a mistake not to. It doesn't so much matter what you do in particular, so long as you have your life. If you haven't had that what *have* you had? This place and these impressions— . . . all my impressions of Chad and of people I've seen at *his* place—well, have had their abundant message for me, have just dropped *that* into my mind. I see it now. I haven't done so enough before—and now I'm old; too old at any rate for what I see. Oh I *do* see, at least; and more than you'd believe or I can express. It's too late. . . . The affair—I mean the affair of life—couldn't, no doubt, have been different for me; for it's at the best a tin mould, either fluted and embossed, with ornamental excrescences, or else smooth and dreadfully plain, into which, a helpless jelly, one's consciousness is poured—so that one 'takes' the form, as the great cook says, and is more or less compactly held by it: one lives in fine as one can. Still, one has the illusion of freedom; therefore don't be like me, without the memory of that illusion. . . . Do what you like so long as you don't make my mistake. For it was a mistake. Live! [23]

Roderick Hudson asks, "What becomes of all . . . the material of thought that life pours into us?" While both Roderick and Rowland advance abstract speculations in answer to the theoretical question, James achieves no concretely dramatized answer in that novel. As a result, his observer's consciousness dissolves into his own omniscience instead of " 'taking' the [narrative] form" itself. Here in *The Ambassadors,* the theoretical question has become a positive statement; the disparate imagery of several speculations has become a single, concretely elaborated image; and a representational system already at work in the novel—as in Strether's meeting with Gloriani—relates a first-person observation on the workings of the mind in general to the dramatized workings of the speaker's own. The speech results directly from those workings, " 'takes' " its form from impressions already shown by James to be molding Strether's view of himself and of Chad. The medium in this case, Strether's cumulative sense of "This place and these impressions," is the abundantly accumulated "message."

True, Strether's argument here is that once the mold of environment has set with age and imparted its pattern to the mind, basic change within that pattern is impossible; or that in any case "it's too late" for him to act upon such change. He still feels more or less compactly held by the Woollett mold. Yet the image of consciousness as "helpless jelly," accepting its form from the variable mold of immediate circumstance, like that in the preface, of the mind as a "green liquid" changing color in the "open cup of *application,"* accounts for changes which *have* occurred in the way Strether sees. What he initially thought of as "the business he had come out on," the job of persuading Chad to return, has become a much more complicated problem—one of "fathoming" not only Chad's relation to Madame de Vionnet, but also his own experience in the altered medium represented by Paris.

When he first sensed the change in Chad, Strether felt that "there was no computing," according to his old assumptions, "what the young man before him would think or feel or say on any subject whatever." Placed in a world of shifting concrete surfaces which "fitfully gleamed," and to which "the imagination, before one could stop it, reacted," he has come to understand that "his mind was a thing that, among . . . [such impressions], he had always needfully to reckon with." Of necessity, Strether now reckons his depth in unfathomed seas by sounding the irregular "flutings" and "excrescences" of the bedrock of experience over which his consciousness flows, rather than "computing" it by moral and intellectual formulae.

From hence emerges the vividly and concretely imagistic quality of his thought. Here, James provides no reports on character and motive and Strether "sees" with greater visual clarity than we find in the mental operations of Rowland Mallett or Isabel Archer. "He was to remember again repeatedly the medal-like Italian face" of Gloriani, whom he also imagines at one point as a "glossy male tiger, magnificently marked." Mrs. Newsome's "whole moral and intellectual being or block," a system of thought worked out in advance of experience and unsusceptible to any surprises experience might offer, presents itself to his mind as "some particularly large iceberg in a cool blue northern sea." The same tendency to visualize rather than immediately to interpret or conclude, to move erratically though not without a certain cumulative accuracy toward conclusions through uncontrolled perception of all available detail, marks the gradual, crucial development in Strether's views of Chad and Madame de Vionnet. The liquid medium of his mind shifts (as in the preface) "from green to red . . . on its way . . . to purple, to black, to yellow," and his sense of each character shifts in response to the drift in his own relation to reality. This process is at once propelled and dramatized by countless "fresh backward, fresh forward, fresh lateral flights" of Strether's imagination.[24]

Thus, whereas Rowland's characteristic state of mind is one of rational clarity, and Isabel's pivotal state of mind is one of still lucidity, Strether's mental state throughout this novel is most often one of partial bewilderment under the assault of impressions which he must sift and filter to fathom the situations from which they arise. Whereas Roderick abstractly imagines the stream of thought as sweeping impressions along, Strether repeatedly feels the "force of the current" of his impressions sweeping him along. The narrative pulse of *The Ambassadors* is in large part the "throb of [Strether's] consciousness" as he strives to keep up with the current, to absorb the constantly inpouring flow of mental data. However successful this effort on his part, and however interesting its results to James and to the reader, Strether never fully comprehends the complexity of the mechanisms involved:

> He couldn't even formulate to himself his being changed and queer; it had taken place, the process, somewhere deep down.[25]

The "fathomless" complexity of the mind, then, is in a sense the true subject of each of the novels. Simplified in *Roderick Hudson* and incompletely projected in *The Portrait of a Lady,* the processes contributing to James's idea of this complexity have indeed "taken place"—become the stuff of drama and passed into the form of continuous narrative—in the fictive psychology of *The Ambassadors.*

Three

That Dual Life: William Dean Howells

> Perhaps . . . in those fastnesses . . . which psychology has not yet explored . . .
>
> *A Modern Instance*

The literary arcs described by the careers as novelists of William Dean Howells and Henry James are strikingly similar in chronology. Each published his first novel in 1871, and whereas Howells published his last, *The Leatherwood God,* in 1916, James's final, unfinished works, *The Ivory Tower* and *The Sense of the Past,* both appeared in 1917, a year after the author's death. The process of development which we observed in James's fictive psychology encompasses more than twenty-five years, from *Roderick Hudson* in 1876 to *The Ambassadors* in 1903, a period virtually if not precisely constituting the entire span of his career. The process of reorientation in Howells's fictive psychology which we shall observe in this chapter, by contrast, encompasses a single decade, from *A Modern Instance* in 1882, through *The Rise of Silas Lapham* in 1885, to *A Hazard of New Fortunes* in 1890.

During these years, and especially between 1885 and 1890, Howells underwent a series of personal crises, and discovered the work of certain other writers (such as Tolstoy and Turgenev, Bellamy and Henry George) who would eventually have considerable influence on his own thought and art. The crises included his involvement in debate over the Haymarket riots of 1886 and the subsequent trial of the Chicago Anarchists, and the death of his daughter. Probably more pertinent to the question of change in his psychological assumptions and techniques, however, was the "vastation" he suffered in 1885, a breakdown in his moral frame of reference as well as a nervous collapse, both having complex relations to the stresses of his situation at the time. This period did not strictly or permanently define Howells's literary interests and identity. It did, however, produce significant intellectual and emotional reorientations, and reconstructed attitudes and feelings which find reflection in the novelist's development between *The Rise of Silas Lapham* and *A Hazard of New Fortunes*. His fictive psychology shows patterns of change more intelligible in this context than in that of the more gradual—though steadier and ultimately more complete—movement characterizing James's.

Bartley Hubbard, Howells's hero in *A Modern Instance,* is two years out of college and editor of a small town newspaper, the *Free Press* of Equity, Maine, when the novel opens. Orphaned when young and brought up in comfortable circumstances by foster parents who pitied and petted him, he has learned to "think of himself as a poor boy . . . winning his way through the world," when actually most of life's obstacles have been smoothed out for him by others. He is ambitious in a vague way for city life and for a profession which he thinks "worthier his powers" than journalism, and so is studying law under Squire Gaylord, the town's leading lawyer. Bartley falls in love with Gaylord's daughter Marcia, but in a curiously passive way since her "impassioned preference for himself" and her eagerness to satisfy his hunger for sympathy, rather than any great depth of feeling on his part, form the real basis of their relationship. They are engaged early in the story, and in the course of describing Bartley's state of mind on this occasion Howells writes:

> Perhaps such a man, in those fastnesses of his nature which psychology has not yet explored, never loses, even in the tenderest transports, the sense of prey as to the girl whose love he has won; but if this is certain, it is also certain that he has transports which are tender, and Bartley now felt his soul melted with affection that was very novel and sweet.[1]

Howells's distinction between unexplored and unspecified psychological "fastnesses" in the abstract, and Bartley's conventionally romantic but more specifically noted "soul" in the concrete, has implications fundamental to the fictive psychology of the novel. He is interested in the fastnesses of Bartley's mind in this particular situation, but can write about them only in generalized and conditional terms ("Perhaps," "such a man," "if this is certain"). He is not without an interest in the process which he attributes to Bartley's "soul," but the point is that Bartley's attitude toward Marcia cannot be defined completely in terms of "tender transports." Yet Howells *does* make a direct statement about these transports of the soul which is more "certain," and which relates more specifically to the narrative of immediate events, than his reference to mental fastnesses, however vague his notion of "melting" as an internal process may be.

This distinction between the obscure fastnesses of the mind and the more familiar responses of the soul or heart implies simultaneously that (1) these psychological recesses lie beyond the novelist's province, at least until psychologists "explore" and map them more thoroughly, and (2) these recesses constitute a dimension of character which the novelist *cannot* afford to overlook completely, however heavily he may rely on a simpler view of the mind as the seat of conventionally categorized romantic responses. In the light of subsequent events, comprising the disintegration of a marriage in which Bartley's stake is basically self-centered, the "sense of prey" is psychologically more relevant than are "tender transports" to Howells's idea of what makes this story new, a *modern* instance departing significantly from sentimental convention. Yet here, at the beginning, he seems uncertain how to bring this relevance into narrative focus. Admittedly the two sides of this psychological coin are bound up together at this point, and admittedly Howells does not wish to tell his entire story in a single early passage. His language, however, suggests a certain tension in his own mind as he approaches the problem of complexity in Bartley's.

A similar uncertainty in Howells's psychological focus is apparent in a passage which occurs almost at the end of the novel. This passage complements the one just examined, and the two provide a frame for discussing *A Modern Instance*. By now Bartley has long since abandoned Marcia, and has recently attempted to divorce her on fraudulent grounds of desertion. They are dead to one another, and Marcia is partly responsible for the situation though she is more sinned against than sinning. She still loves her mistaken idea of what Bartley once was, however, and in some obscure sense blames herself for everything that has happened. After years of declining fortunes and moral deterioration Bartley is shot to death in Whited Sepulchre, Arizona, by a man whose domestic affairs he chooses to notice in the scurrilous newspaper he has sunk to editing. When Marcia learns of this death, Howells tells us:

> Marcia had been widowed so long before that this event could make no outward change in her. What inner change, if any, it wrought, is one of those facts which fiction must seek in vain to disclose. But if love such as hers had been did not deny his end the pang of a fresh grief, we may be sure that her sorrow was not unmixed with self-accusal . . .[2]

"Inner change" in Marcia's mind, like the "fastnesses" of Bartley's, is something simultaneously inaccessible and interesting to Howells. He comments directly on the absence of any visible change, on the fact that Bartley had in a sense died long before, but his approach to the question of internal process is again tentative and conditional. He suggests that even if such a process occurred he would be unprepared (and perhaps unqualified) to analyze it in detail. Moreover, the language of his conditional speculation on the subject, in which he tells us what "we may [at least] be sure" of for narrative purposes, evokes the idea of mind as soul more readily than that of remote mental fastnesses. Yet Howells also refers to inner change in Marcia as a "fact," something as real as the presence or absence of outward change, although lying beyond the usual reach of fiction. And if he feels, at this point, that the novelist must seek in vain to reveal the nature of inner change, *we* feel that Howells is beginning to move toward a conviction that the novelist must seek none the less to discover some means of doing so.

The tension apparent in both of these passages, between the idea that certain psychological considerations must necessarily remain "blank" to the writer of fiction and a sense that the same considerations are somehow forcing their own way into the picture, pervades the entire work. After retiring on the night of his engagement to Marcia, for example, Bartley muses over the day's impressions and events, his mind in "a confusion of pleasure":

> It is possible that as he drowsed, at last, there floated airily through the consciousness which was melting and dispersing itself before the approach of sleep, an intimation from somewhere to some one that perhaps the affair need not be considered too seriously. But in that mysterious limbo one cannot be sure of what is thought and what is dreamed . . .[3]

The most definitely reportable element of this sequence is the melting and dispersing of Bartley's consciousness into the "mysterious limbo" of approaching sleep. "Melting and dispersing itself" suggests the self-generating flow and freely mingling currents of a mental stream, and recalls from James's *Roderick Hudson* the notion of impressions "melting like water into water." The same phrase, however, implies that Bartley's consciousness is accessible to Howells only in what he later calls its "sane and waking state," that it melts from the view of the novelist with the coming of sleep to the character and ceases to be Howells's narrative responsibility just as it ceases to be Bartley's moral responsibility. (Howells tells us as the passage continues that Bartley "always acquitted himself, and probably with justice, of any [conscious] want of seriousness.") "Mysterious limbo" suggests the penumbral area of semi-awareness at the edge of a Jamesian character's mental stream, though here it also reinforces the sense of inaccessibility to the narrative eye.

Despite its ambiguity, this description of the drift of Bartley's mind toward sleep refers to an unquestioned psychological occurrence. Howells allows only the "possibility," by contrast, that the vague and formless intimation of Bartley's lack of serious commitment "floated airily through" his mind. Because it *is* a possibility rather than a narrative certainty, and because it occurs in a mysterious mental limbo if indeed it occurs at all, Howells undertakes to represent this intimation in only the most minimal way. Its "floating" motion accords with the idea of melting and dispersing thought, but beyond this we learn only that it cannot be further defined because "one cannot be sure of what is thought and what is dreamed" on the frontier of sleep. If he were able to assign this psychic event to the realm of thought—implying rational control and moral responsibility—Howells would probably pay at least somewhat more detailed attention to it. Were he able to assign it to the realm of dream—implying neither control nor responsibility, nor indeed any real significance for the immediate situation—he would be free to ignore it altogether, or perhaps to treat it more fully *as* a dream according to his own ideas about such phenomena. As it is, however, the novelist himself "cannot be sure" and the mental process itself remains conditionally represented and oddly unlocated, even with reference to the mind in which it possibly occurs (coming "from somewhere to some one"). Bartley's uncertainty in the matter is admittedly part of Howells's ironic point: his lack of seriousness is precisely what will destroy the marriage and eventually Bartley himself. Howells's reluctance to take on the representational problem posed by this uncertainty, however, seems to proceed from an artistic uncertainty of his own. Whereas James tends to deal with penumbral awareness as a means toward increased specificity and "complication" in his fictive psychology, Howells places an internal process beyond his own representational reach in a "mysterious limbo" for the purpose of *not* confronting it directly or in detail.

In a slightly later passage, Howells gives further expression to this uncertainty. During a quarrel in the *Free Press* office with his copy boy Henry Bird over the merits (relative to those of Marcia Gaylord) of Hannah Morrison, whom Henry loves and with whose affections Bartley had trifled earlier, the copy boy strikes his employer an ineffectual blow:

> The demons, whatever they were, of anger, remorse, pride, shame, were at work in Bartley's heart too, and he returned the blow as instantly as if Bird's touch had set the mechanism of his arm in motion. In contempt of the other's weakness he struck with the flat of his hand; but the blow was enough. Bird fell headlong, and . . . lay senseless.
>
> Bartley hung over the boy with such a terror in his soul as he had never had before. He believed that he had killed him, and in this conviction came with the simultaneity of events in dreams the sense of all his blame. . . . Amidst the anguish of his self-condemnation the need to conceal what he had done occurred to him. He . . . turned to the door and locked it, and the lie by which he should escape sprang to his tongue. "He died in a fit." He almost believed it as it

> murmured itself from his lips. There was no mark, no bruise, nothing to show that he had touched the boy. Suddenly he felt the lie choke him. He pulled down the window to let in the fresh air, and this pure breath of heaven blew into his darkened spirit and lifted there a little the vapors which were thickening in it.[4]

Then, as the boy slowly recovers and Bartley suffers from a sense of "outlawry" although the incident is hushed up by Squire Gaylord and the doctor attending Bird,

> . . . he discovered in himself that dual life of which everyone who sins or sorrows is sooner or later aware: that strange separation of the intellectual activity from the suffering of the soul, by which the mind toils on in a sort of ironical indifference to the pangs that wring the heart; the realization that, in some ways, his brain can get on perfectly well without his conscience.[5]

The "mechanism" of Bartley's response to the blow he received is a new note in Howells's fictive psychology, however faintly sounded here. As for the psychological force behind the mechanism, Howells once again "cannot be sure." He is certain, on the one hand, that Bartley's act is not the literal work of literal "demons," personified moral abstractions including two of the seven deadly sins. He is uncertain, on the other, how otherwise to represent the process involved. "Whatever they [really] were" in psychological terms, he settles for "demons," and, like Holmes in *The Guardian Angel,* can "only tell what happened" externally: "he returned the blow."

The demons having been at work in Bartley's "heart," terror at the thought of having killed the boy now afflicts his "soul." The first reaction which consciously absorbs him is the "sense of all his blame." He analyzes this introspectively during the subsequent ellipsis. Beneath the conscious and redeeming anguish of his moral self-analysis, the instincts of self-preservation assert themselves in Bartley's mind. The need to conceal and the lie by which to escape occur to him and "spring" into the action of a locked door or a spoken thought as mechanically as the blow itself, the lie even "murmuring itself," without his conscious agency, to his moral sense, which he almost manages to deceive.

Yet Howells accounts for the impact of this lie on his character's consciousness in terms strongly reminiscent of Mrs. Stowe's fictive psychology in *Uncle Tom's Cabin.* Several of James's characters open figurative doors or windows in their minds to admit air whose potential for action upon their mental processes rests ultimately on considerations of environmental change. The door "suddenly opened . . . to agitation" in Isabel's mind at the beginning of her vigil in the first version of the *Portrait,* and the windows thrown open to the "sun of a clime not marked in [Strether's] old geography," are particularly striking examples. Here Bartley opens a literal window letting in literal air, which Howells proceeds to imagine as very nearly literal influence from the supernatural, the "pure breath of heaven" dispelling spiritual darkness and vapors. Falsehood in the abstract chokes Bartley; moral truth in the abstract revives him. In neither case, as far as this particular part of the passage is concerned, does Howells conceive of the process as explicitly psychological in nature.

But in the next passage the novelist begins to confront the problem of the relation between divergent forces within his fictive psychology. The immediately intended point is simply that Bartley continues to function professionally and indeed finds solace in his work. Nevertheless, Howells himself is discovering in theory, if not yet extensively demonstrating in narrative fact, that psychological representation "can get on perfectly well without"—need not always be projected as—the representation of moral self-consciousness or of the controlling influence of abstract moral values. In *Roderick Hudson,* Roderick says to Rowland in the course of a typically theoretical discussion of free will:

> There are all kinds of uncanny underhand currents moving to and fro between one's will and the rest of one—one's imagination in particular. People talk as if the two things were essentially distinct; on different sides of one's organism, like the heart and the liver. Mine, I know—that is my imagination and my conscience—are much nearer together.[6]

Roderick expresses in diagrammatic terms one of the points which James intends to dramatize, but fails to dramatize effectively, in the novel: that mental process *and* moral insight are matters of subtly moving "currents," and not the mutually exclusive functions of totally different faculties. Whereas the unanalyzed dictates of Nora's conscience determine the action in *Watch and Ward,* and the carefully traced movements of Strether's imagination "account for everything" in *The Ambassadors,* James is midway between these points in *Roderick.* Psychological representation has become a possible means of exploring a moral problem, instead of being rendered irrelevant by a set of moral assumptions which themselves account for all change. Here, in *A Modern Instance,* Howells arrives at a somewhat similar conceptual milestone, although he expresses it differently. While distinguishing between "conscience" and "brain," he suggests that he is as much concerned artistically with the latter as with the former, which was not the case in *A Chance Acquaintance.* He himself finds this "strange," a term we have come to recognize as a sign of simultaneous interest in and uncertainty about psychological subject matter; "uncanny" in the passage from *Roderick* strikes a similar note. *A Modern Instance* shows Howells beginning to pursue this interest and to confront the representational problems it entails.

Howells's later work does not exhibit a linear and continuous development, such as we find in James's fiction, from an abstractly formulated "geometry" of psychological representation toward the concretely dramatized "molding" of narrative by a specific consciousness. Nor do Howells's novels move as evenly from circumscription by moral assumptions in an apprentice work to morally open-ended concern with the process of "seeing" in a mature work. Howell's fictive psychology, like his hero in *A Modern Instance,* contains a "dual life" which persists into the successive stages of his art. This process carries into changing configurations, but never truly resolves, the elements of conflict in the narrative demands of "conscience" and "brain." It also perpetuates, while pressing into increasingly sophisticated artistic form, the tension between fascination with and bafflement by the "fastnesses" of the mind. What Howells says of his hero in *The Rise of Silas Lapham,* we might say of the novelist himself as he develops and modifies assumptions and techniques without the aid of a general plan of psychological representation such as James had:

> He had the idea, but it floated vague, elusive, in his brain. He looked about as if for something to precipitate it in tangible shape.[7]

In *The Rise of Silas Lapham,* indeed, considerations of moral change and psychological process are quite closely identified, the latter in many respects solidly subordinate to the former. The story is about the efforts of Silas Lapham, a *nouveau riche* paint manufacturer from rural Vermont, to establish himself and his family in Boston society, which is represented by the Brahmin family of Bromfield Corey. Howells's best efforts to account for the operations of Lapham's mind, however, occur in connection with the two moral crises which frame (both textually and thematically) the record of his experience amid changed conditions in Boston. The first crisis is created when Lapham, before the novel begins, forces his partner (whose capital had previously saved the company) out of the business. He does this to gain full control of their enterprise before its value soars. Lapham attributes this act to morally neutral "business ferocity," insisting that "It's a thing that's done every day" and that his conscience is clear. Moral goading from his wife Persis, certified to the reader by Howells as sound guidance and eventually recognized as such by Silas, sets up interior reverberations which echo throughout the developing narrative. The second crisis culminates in Lapham's climactic refusal to sell worthless property through the agency of his former partner to an unsuspecting syndicate, even though he would be legally secure and the intermediate profit to the man he originally wronged would salve his conscience. His moral rise ensures his financial ruin—the projected killing was his own last hope for recouping heavy losses through speculation—and he retreats to the virtuous simplicity of the land from which he came.

An early passage shows the foundation upon which psychological representation in this work rests:

> . . . [Persis's] zeal and courage formed the spring of [Silas's] enterprise. In that affair of the partnership she had tried to be his conscience, but perhaps she would have defended him if he had accused himself; it was one of those things in this life which seem destined to await justice, or at least judgment, in the next. As he said, Lapham had dealt fairly by his partner in money; he had let Rogers take more money out of the business than he put into it; he had, as he said, simply forced out of it a timid and inefficient participant in advantages which he had created. But Lapham had not created them all. He had been dependent at one time on his partner's capital. It was a moment of terrible trial. Happy is the man for ever after who can choose the ideal, the unselfish part in such an exigency! Lapham could not rise to it. He did what he could maintain to be perfectly fair. That wrong, if any, seemed to be condoned to him, except when from time to time his wife brought it up. Then all the question stung and burned anew, and had to be reasoned out and put away once more. It seemed to have an inextinguishable vitality. It slept but it did not die.[8]

This passage is at once a simple exposition, an omniscient summary of past events, and an attempt to account analytically for the origins, now long past, of a sequence of mental events still very much alive to Howells. Earlier, he says of the gradual emergence of Lapham's Back Bay mansion from blueprinted abstraction toward tangible reality: "The beginnings of the process . . . are so obscure that it would be almost impossible to trace them. But it all happened. . . ." Here, too, the psychological seeds of Lapham's prior act and presently unacknowledged guilt prove almost impossible for Howells to trace in detail; he falls back on a factual outline of how "it all happened." Yet there are certain elements of psychological analysis.

From the outset, Persis's moral influence, what Howells elsewhere calls her capacity for knowing and doing "what was wise and right," is implied as a dramatically functioning factor—a "spring"—in Silas's inward life, just as her general fortitude is a supporting factor in his actual enterprise. Although unable, in this instance, to withstand the force of his "business ferocity" (a force conventionally given here, as is the moral superiority on Persis's part to which it ultimately yields), Persis's influence is what keeps the moral question "stinging and burning anew" in Lapham's mind. Howells neither dramatizes nor specifically examines these interior sensations at this point. Nor does he demonstrate the process of choice involved in Lapham's "terrible moment of trial," commenting on the situation instead through an abstract maxim beginning "Happy is the man. . . ." He introduces both the process and the inward sensations, however, as psychological facts whose full impact remains to be felt in the novel.

Immediately before this passage Howells does dramatize, through an extended dialogue with virtually no intrusion on his part, one case of the problem's being "reasoned out and put away once more" by the couple. The portrayal amounts to formal debate between fixed positions on the issue, and the reasoning process involved is one of recitation rather than one of internal inquiry. But

Howells's omniscience momentarily gives way, for a more convincingly psychological purpose. Although he tends to represent the moral problem as clear-cut, and to insist on the clarity of Persis's moral vision from the start, he is also concerned with representing the difficulty, the "exigency" of Lapham's and her own engagement with the problem as plausible. Thus he shades the statement beginning "it was one of those things . . ." toward Persis's point of view without designating it as her idea or literal statement. Similarly, in the repeated phrase "as he said," Howells concurs with two statements approximating (albeit in the third person) Silas's own accumulated thought on the subject, before going on to revise that view for the reader: "But Lapham had not created them all." We therefore have a sense, after reading the passage, of a tension built up by processes which are largely unrepresented, yet which are present below the narrative surface and potentially available in greater detail. Howells's fictive psychology in *Silas Lapham,* seemingly more archaic than in *A Modern Instance,* is, like Lapham's dilemma, asleep but by no means dead.

We may observe it in its waking state during Lapham's second "moment of terrible trial," near the end of the novel. In this scene his material doom is sealed and his moral rise is crowned, and the narrative action is climaxed. Having been approached by Rogers with the land scheme, and having heard Rogers claim that Lapham owes it to him to sell rather than to himself not to sell, Silas painfully ponders his decision, "trying to drop another anchor for a fresh clutch on his underlying principles":

> Lapham stole a troubled glance at his wife, and saw that there was no help in her. Whether she was daunted and confused in her own conscience by the outcome, so evil and disastrous, of the reparation to Rogers which she had forced her husband to make, or whether her perceptions had been blunted and darkened by the appeals which Rogers now used, it would be difficult to say. Probably there was a

mixture of both causes in the effect which her husband felt in her. . . .

Lapham glanced again at his wife; her head had fallen; he could see that she was so rooted in her old remorse for that questionable act of his, amply and more than fully atoned for since, that she was helpless, now in the crucial moment, when he had the utmost need of her insight. He had counted upon her; he perceived now that when he had thought it was for him alone to decide, he had counted upon her just spirit to stay his own in its struggle to be just. . . . He swallowed the lump that rose in his throat, the self-pity, the pity for her, the despair, and said gently, "I guess you better go to bed, Persis. It's pretty late." . . . She went out of the door, and left him with his tempter. . . .

"The question is," [said Rogers,] "Will you sell, and, if so, what is your figure? You have got nothing whatever to do with it after you've sold."

It was perfectly true. Any lawyer would have told him the same. He could not help admiring Rogers for his ingenuity, and every selfish interest of his nature joined with many obvious duties to urge him to consent. He did not see why he should refuse. . . .

"Can't you see that you will not be responsible for what happens after you have sold?" [asked Rogers.]

"No, I *can't* see that; but if I can by morning, I'll sell." . . . [Rogers leaves.]

"Want I should come down and talk with you?" [asked Persis.]

"No," answered Lapham, in the proud bitterness which his isolation brought, "you couldn't do any good."

He went in and shut the door, and by and by his wife heard him begin walking up and down; and then the rest of the night she lay awake and listened to him walking up and down. But when the first light whitened the window, the words of the Scripture came into her mind: "And there wrestled a man with him until the breaking of the day." [9]

The length of this sequence in relation to most passages already discussed, along with the fact that it is a patchwork of elements and modes only some of which contribute directly to the portrayal of Lapham's mind, clearly demonstrates Howells's disinterest in the unbroken "view from within," in the Jamesian sense. He intrudes to report Silas's thoughts (as in the second paragraph) and to speculate abstractly on the nature of Persis's mental response to the situation (as in the first), not to mention his intrusion for the purpose of basic exposition and the management of dialogue. He also leaves the crucial phase of Lapham's interior process—a nightlong vigil of searching self-analysis which, like Isabel Archer's, is intended by the novelist to enable the character to "see" with greater inward clarity—off the narrative stage altogether. During this vigil we cannot watch Lapham himself, far less the detailed movements of his mind, except through the sound of his footsteps which Persis hears throughout the night. We can sense the decisive turn in his deliberations only through "the words of the Scripture" which come into *her* mind, formally quoted as frequently happens in *Uncle Tom's Cabin,* and conventionally reflected in the "first light" coming through her window. This recalls the supernatural intervention in the mechanics of moral decision in Mrs. Stowe's novel. Persis, indeed, although helpless to solve Lapham's problem, continues to exert moral influence over the workings of his mind. She hovers wakefully above him all night, an almost literally angelic presence in opposition to the "tempter" below.

Yet Howells *is* concerned, despite the absence of Jamesian closeness and continuity from his psychological attention, with both the organic sequence and the operational complexities of his characters' minds. As in *A Modern Instance,* he finds it "difficult to say" just what has occurred in Persis's mind to make her withdraw her active assistance "now in the crucial moment," and is reluctant to commit himself on the question of whether it is a matter of "confused conscience" or one of "darkened perception." Similar as these may be in the terms of this novel's fictive psychology, he assumes some sort of complex interaction, an uncanny current such as James imagines in *Roderick Hudson* to be moving between figurative heart and liver: "Probably there was a mixture." Moreover, these elements of process are "causes" in a sequence of psychological cause and effect the primary narrative "effect" of which is Lapham's sense of his wife's withdrawal. Only because he feels dismay at her refusal to advise him does Silas arrive at his perception, in the second paragraph, of how completely he had counted upon her in the past. Hence, too, "the self-pity, the pity for her, the despair" which Howells leaves unexamined and but minimally dramatized in Lapham's "lump" of emotion, but which comprise his interior drift toward true confrontation with "The question."

Business ferocity asserts itself in Silas's mind, together with duties of a practical rather than a moral nature—"obvious," environmentally imposed duties of survival for himself and those dependent on him—in response to Rogers's point of view on this question. He instinctively recognizes the security offered by a legalistic solution to the situation. Although the statement, "It was perfectly true," is Howells's, because it is brief and otherwise free of authorial accoutrements it suggests a spontaneous insight within Lapham's mind. He also warms involuntarily to the ingenuity of the plan, and feels strong "urgings" in its favor from his drive toward material well-being and accommodation to circumstances. Through the lens of this drive, which Lapham defends at various points in the story but which Howells condemns here, "He did not see why he should refuse." The "anchor" of his conscience, securing to the bedrock of "principle" a mind afloat on the sea of new experience and adrift in the currents of changed conditions, has slipped with the pull of those currents.

It has not altogether lost its "clutch," however, for Silas is also unable to "see that [he] will not be responsible." We are not shown the process of vision through which he comes to see that he *would* be responsible, through which conscience reaffirms its control over an adaptive brain, a brain potentially answerable to other than moral law. The fact that Howells assumes and values such control in this novel, along with his representational uncertainties regarding mental process here and in earlier works, probably accounts for that. We have, nevertheless, seen something of the psychological movement toward a situation in which conscience is "confused" and moral perception "blunted and darkened" by unacknowledged forces both within and without the character's consciousness. We have glimpsed a literary situation in which the slippage of a mental anchor, the process of its being cast anew, and perhaps of its being exchanged for a different sort of mooring to reality—a sea anchor suspended in the fluid medium of experience and allowing for drift while maintaining equilibrium—might take on more narrative importance than if it were re-embedded in "underlying" and unchanging values.

Such processes are implicitly important in *A Modern Instance,* but Bartley Hubbard's interior disintegration, like Roderick Hudson's, fails of continuous dramatization. In *The Rise of Silas Lapham* as well, such processes remain latent at best. Howells is concerned with their operation "in the particular connexion" within Silas's mind—hence the mixture of exposition and dialogue with psychological observation in the passage above. But he defines this concern in even less explicitly psychological terms than those framing his more theoretical interest in Bartley's inner change. In *A Hazard of New Fortunes,* however, he explores these processes more fully, and brings more supple representational skills to bear on the relation between moral consciousness and physical environment, between inflexible conscience and adaptive brain.

One scene in particular from *A Hazard of New Fortunes* invites comparison with the scene just discussed from *The Rise of Silas Lapham.* This situation, too, constitutes a "moment of terrible trial" for the hero, Basil March, and although Howells this time omits the melodramatic phrase, he is very much concerned with the "terror" in March's mind as he confronts a crucial decision. Dissatisfied with the placidity of life in Boston, he has moved with his wife and children to "vast, . . . shapeless" New York, a city which he finds exciting as well as obscurely frightening. In New York, March becomes the editor of a new literary magazine called *Every Other Week*. Conceived and promoted by a man named Fulkerson, the magazine is backed by Jacob Dryfoos, a latter-day Silas Lapham whose fortune derives from the discovery of natural gas on his native Midwestern farmlands. Like Lapham, Dryfoos has come to the city to establish his family in society, as well as to manage his financial interests. Out of charity as well as out of growing interest in his ideas, March arranges for Lindau, an impoverished German socialist, to join the staff of *Every Other Week* (and thus indirectly to work for the capitalist Dryfoos). Tension between Lindau and Dryfoos grows, as does March's sympathy with, if not conversion to, Lindau's social and economic outlook. When Dryfoos orders him to fire Lindau, March insists that he is responsible to Fulkerson in such matters and refuses to comply. Dryfoos leaves in a rage, and Howells focuses on the reverberations of this encounter in March's mind:

> He could not have taken any ground in relation to Dryfoos but that which he held, and he felt satisfied that he was right in refusing to receive instructions or commands from him. Yet somehow he was not satisfied with the whole affair, and not merely because his present triumph threatened his final advantage, but because he felt that in his heat he had hardly done justice to Dryfoos's rights in the matter; it did not quite console him to reflect that Dryfoos had himself made it impossible. He was tempted to go home and tell his wife what had happened, and begin his preparations for the future at once. But he resisted this weakness and kept mechanically

> about his work, opening the letters and manuscripts before him, with that curious double action of the mind common in men of vivid imaginations.[10]

Then, after Fulkerson tries and fails to persuade March to give in, and March threatens to resign if not backed against Dryfoos, Howells resumes the analysis of his hero's consciousness:

> His indignation kept him hot in his purpose to suffer any consequences rather than submit to the dictation of a man like Dryfoos; . . . at the same time his heart ached with foreboding. It was not merely the work in which he had constantly grown happier that he saw taken from him; but he felt the misery of the man who stakes the security and plenty and peace of home upon some cast, and knows that losing will sweep from him most that most men find sweet and pleasant in life. He faced the fact, which no good man can front without terror, that he was risking the support of his family, and for a point of pride, of honour, which perhaps he had no right to consider in view of the possible adversity. . . . His indignation was shot with abject impulses to go back and tell Fulkerson that it was all right, and that he gave up.[11]

March's interior struggle to maintain his hold on the moral ground at stake in this situation is considerably more complex than Lapham's. Howells represents the drag of a moral anchor under pressure from environmental waves more fully here than in the earlier work. At the beginning, we find March in a moral stance with which he is consciously "satisfied," whereas Lapham's psychological efforts are directed wholly toward the achievement of such a stance, and for March this satisfaction "that he was right" is an inadequate solution to the problem. Indeed, it creates the problem which is the passage's main concern: the problem of whether or not he has another sort of "right" to risk "possible adversity" for a point of honor. Such adversity is relatively harmless in *Silas Lapham;* Silas simply retreats to rural life, with its implied moral security, and no question of survival ever arises. Here, however, the practical problem of survival under adverse circumstances inspires real "terror" in March, the more so because his "goodness" consists in his ability to "face the [environmental] fact" as well as the abstract moral issue.

Howells refers to this terror in a generalized statement which avoids actual representation of the interior sensation, just as the statement "Happy is the man . . . who can choose the ideal" in *Silas Lapham* avoids representation of the process of choice. Such statements bespeak a mind less attuned to observing particular psychological differences than to theorizing about broad psychological patterns. Nevertheless, he dramatizes the interweaving of fear with moral indignation in the flow of March's mind throughout the passage, and he does so in some detail. March's dissatisfaction with the initial encounter with Dryfoos stems in part from a reasoned sense of not having adequately recognized Dryfoos's point of view. We get less authorial help here than in *Silas Lapham* toward evaluating opposed viewpoints, and March, like Strether, must work his mental way through various and often morally mixed possibilities. His internal uneasiness also stems from the threat he perceives to his material advantage in his moral triumph. "Reflection" does little to ease his mind, and is countered by the "temptation" to enact his fear by assuming the worst and beginning to look for another position. Lapham confronts *his* tempter in the person of Rogers, and wrestles introspectively with the choice he is offered throughout a whole night. March's temptation is a momentary thrust of panic, an instinctive movement toward material security which occurs before he is fully aware of it, as the passive construction suggests.

March consciously resists this movement, which Howells labels a weakness, just as he labels as selfish the inclination in Silas toward selling, but it remains a psychological "fact" which will not submit to conscious control. His "heart"—here a source of survival instinct—"aches with foreboding" at the thought of consequences which his moral sense is prepared to accept. His "misery" —like his terror a quality abstractly named yet concretely shown by Howells—springs from the sudden awareness that much more than a plot of moral ground is at stake. His consciousness is literally shot through with impulses such as these, impulses which Howells condemns as "abject," but which he also acknowledges as being intrinsically important to the narrative.

Although by no means as direct and continuous a transcript of mental proceedings as James makes Isabel's vigil, this narrative of March's mind is more evenly sustained and more closely observant than either of the passages from *The Rise of Silas Lapham.* The paragraphs treated here as a single sequence are separated by an interval of dialogue and action, but neither is itself broken up in the manner of the long section from the earlier work. The action of these paragraphs is exclusively the action of the mind. Sentence structure, which in *Silas Lapham* must allow for rapid changes in narrative mode and is elaborately formal and complex, remains complex in this novel. Here, however, it more nearly resembles the occasionally turgid but generally fluid currents of Jamesian syntax in the *Portrait* and *The Ambassadors.* Commas are fewer than in *Silas Lapham,* and semicolons create a sense of linkage and continuity in the psychological record, rather than a sense of formalized rhetoric.

Howells tends, as we have noticed, to cast key observations about the nature of his characters' interior processes in the form of implied generalizations which avoid representing those processes "in the particular connexion." This passage tends to dramatize these generalizations, and although the narrator's third-person omniscience is unvarying, he focuses it evenly on March's own point of view. Indeed, because he is recording a "double" process, combining a character's conscious reflection with impulses of which the character is neither fully aware nor in conscious control,

Howells's blend of analysis from March's angle of vision with more detached, even scientifically removed commentary from his own is quite appropriate.

This sequence thus illustrates that "curious double action of the mind" to which the novelist refers—once again in an abstract generalization—at the end of the first paragraph. In *A Modern Instance* he called it "that dual life . . . that strange separation of the intellectual activity from the suffering of the soul." In both novels the immediate point is a limited one; Basil, like Bartley, functions "mechanically" while inwardly absorbed in other matters. As in the earlier case, however, Howells's language has broader implications for his fictive psychology. What was "strange," remote, and therefore beyond or only peripherally within his representational powers, has become more accessibly "curious," and therefore the subject of more immediate interest as well as the object of more intensive representational effort. Bartley's vaguely conceived mental life and the abstractly imagined separation of his mental and moral faculties have been fused into the "action" of March's mind, an action more carefully observed and more extensively dramatized than in Howells's earlier writings. Conscience and brain, James's "heart" and "liver," have become aspects (though still sometimes contradictory) of a single process, which is available to the writer through psychological observation, and to the reader through psychological representation.

We noticed a tendency in James's later fiction toward resolution of conflict on the basis of enlarged awareness in a central perceiver, of such a character's "seeing" the true nature of his experience whether or not it ends happily or even conclusively. Consciousness itself takes on a kind of moral value in *The Portrait of a Lady* and *The Ambassadors,* replacing the moral absolutes of the earlier works, just as James's increasingly intensive representation of consciousness in these novels takes on increasing esthetic importance. "The ordeal of consciousness" [12] produces in Isabel Archer a truer sense of reality than she originally possessed, and although that reality is bleak there is value in her having come to see it more clearly. "The religion of consciousness" [13] becomes for Lambert Strether, as indeed for James himself, the source of meaning and value in experience, and in the fictive re-creation of experience.

We also find in Howells's mature fiction a suggestion of the resolution of fictive issues on psychological grounds, although it is not so coherent a dramatization as James's. Howells seems to cast his artistic lot with a final interior state which represents a character's accumulated experience, but does not necessarily represent a clarified view of that experience. Such a state is the result of action upon, rather than of action within, the character's mind, and must therefore be carefully observed from without rather than carefully constructed from within.

Thus, in *A Hazard of New Fortunes,* after Fulkerson has backed March against Dryfoos and Lindau has left the literary magazine because of his own moral aversion to the gas millionaire, Dryfoos departs for Europe, a disillusioned man further defeated by the death of his son during a strike. He cannot return to rural life as Lapham does; gas-wells have ruined the land, which in any event now belongs to Standard Oil. Howells's concern in this novel for psychological continuity prevents any sudden change in values such as that which Lapham undergoes. The dramatized fact of Dryfoos's final state—disillusionment because his financial power failed to control the world around him, but disillusionment devoid of enlarged understanding—constitutes the resolution of his character. Similarly, March, who is perplexed by the "riddle of the painful earth" throughout the novel, remains so at the end, whatever he has learned from his experience. He has felt the pain—the "terror" of possible adversity as a result of a moral act—but the riddle itself is not presented by Howells for solution in this work.

March, therefore, cannot really answer his wife when she asks, "Then what *is* it that changes us?" in response to his remark that Dryfoos's experience has not changed his outlook. He can only say something indicative of the difference in fictive psychology between this book and *Uncle Tom's Cabin,* a novel which we saw to be closely related in its psychology to Howells's earliest fiction: "Well, it won't do to say, the Holy Spirit indwelling. That would sound like cant at this day." What he goes on to suggest by way of a positive answer, nevertheless, contains a hint of a different sort of determinism, of a shaping force more biological than spiritual:

> I suppose I should have to say that we didn't change at all. We develop. There's the making of several characters in each of us; we *are* several characters, and sometimes this character has the lead in us, and sometimes that. . . . The growth in one direction has stopped; it's begun in another; that's all. . . .
>
> "Basil! Basil!" cried his wife. "This is fatalism!" [14]

March manages to calm his wife's fears on this account, but a latent sense of determinism remains in the fictive psychology of the novel. We shall find that this determinism becomes overt in the work of a young writer whose career was of particular interest to Howells, and who published his first novel only three years after *A Hazard of New Fortunes* appeared: Stephen Crane.

Four

The Laws of Life: Stephen Crane

His accumulated thought upon such
subjects was used to form scenes.
The Red Badge of Courage

Crane's fiction presents special opportunities and special problems. Indeed, in the patterns of fictive psychology which we find in his work, as in the shape of his career and life, he might be called what James was to call his hero in the "Preface to *Roderick Hudson*": a "morbidly special case." James uses the phrase primarily to describe his own failure to relieve the implausible suddenness of Roderick's disintegration, the totality of his fatal subjection to "temperament," by tracing its interior phases more evenly and continuously. Regarding Crane's experience and achievement the phrase has a more literal ring. "Morbidity" is not the cornerstone of his literary imagination, particularly regarding psychological representation, even though there are frequent images of death and decay in his stories, and their impact on the minds of his characters is often important. Crane's importance, for our discussion, does not lie in the isolated idiosyncrasy of his psychological conceptions and portrayals. His work contains elements of continuity, and elements of connecting rather than of isolating contrast, with problems already discussed in the works of James and Howells, and to be discussed in those of Norris and Dreiser. Nevertheless, the rhythm of his artistic life, the pace and even the nature of change in his fictive psychology, are profoundly different from the development and growth seen in the lengthier, more prolific careers of James and Howells. This difference requires that we construct an analytical case for Crane within the framework of conditions distinguishing his career from theirs.

Born in 1871 (the year James published *Watch and Ward*) and dead of tuberculosis in 1900 (the year Dreiser's *Sister Carrie* first appeared), Crane produced virtually all his important work during the last eight years of his life. *Maggie: A Girl of the Streets,* his privately issued and commercially unsuccessful first effort, and *The Red Badge of Courage,* the novel which established his reputation and upon which it still largely rests, appeared in 1893 and 1895 respectively, and were composed even closer to one another in time. These works represent the range of his psychological assumptions and techniques as well as any other comparisons possible among his stories. Clearly the process of literary development is different in its operations from the gradual evolutions apparent in the accumulated works of James or Howells (however distinct the arcs described by *their* careers may be). This need not concern us extensively: no comprehensive theory of development in Crane's art is at stake here. It is worth noting, however, that analyzing change in Crane's fictive psychology is more like perceiving the interlocked facets of a crystal under changing light than like tracing the gradual process of the crystal's formation. His talent for psychological representation, like his literary life as a whole, seems more explosive than evolutional.

Crane's logic in *Maggie,* when this work is viewed as a whole, would seem to require that the title character be from the very beginning a demoralized product of destructive environment. Maggie Johnson, however, appears at the story's start an almost archetypal innocent, and the workings of her mind resemble those of earlier heroines to a certain degree. She "blossoms in a mud-puddle," to be sure, and curses vigorously when cuffed; yet she is unusual, "a most rare and wonderful production of a tenement district, a pretty girl. None of the dirt of Rum Alley seemed to be in her veins." In the numbing atmosphere of a New York City slum of that name, an atmosphere summed up in the almost choral repetition of "Ah, what d' hell!" by her brother Jimmie and his bartender friend Pete, she is able to dream of an "ideal man" (and Crane to describe her reverie) in terms suggestive of an earlier mode:

> Her dim thoughts were often searching for far-away lands where the little hills sing together in the morning. Under the trees of her dream-gardens there had always walked a lover.[1]

Crane, of course, intends to show by means of irony that the dream is kindled in Maggie's mind by the bravado of Pete's "Ah, what d' hell!" At this point in his career, he is more interested in such sharp but essentially simple ironies than he is in the possibility that his characters' thoughts might provide him with more complex narrative material. His reliance on a Biblical passage, "where the little hills sing together in the morning," enforces the ironic contrast between Rum Alley and "dream-gardens," and between Pete (whom Maggie is actually thinking of here as "ideal") and the abstract "lover," rather than brings her "dim"—and surely less literate—thought process itself directly into the narrative. Indeed, Crane's use of Biblical language in reference to Maggie's thought contains an element of authorial commentary not altogether unrelated to Mrs. Stowe's scriptural glosses on her characters' minds, though here it is undidactic and thus different in its rhetorical context.

Nor is the "rare and wonderful" innocence which Maggie briefly possesses in a world in which, as Crane inscribed in a first-edition copy he sent to Hamlin Garland, "environment is a tremendous thing in the world and frequently shapes lives regardless," [2] without its implications for his initial assumptions about her mind. Crane's environmentalism (he calls it a "theory" in the same inscription) is drastically foreshortened in this first novel, and depends for its effect on a subject who is in some respects foreshortened as well. It is almost as if Crane were deliberately introducing an earlier literary type, who appears "rare" because she is initially inexplicable in terms of his theory, and saying "Watch and see what reality as I know it to be will do to your heroine." Maggie, of course, is by no means the sentimental stereotype—complete with conventional moral reflexes in place of observable mental processes—transported bodily to Rum Alley from, say, an early novel by Howells. She knows precisely what Jimmie means when, shortly after we are told that she has "none of the dirt of Rum Alley . . . in her veins," he tells her she must either "go on d' toif er go t' work!" Nevertheless, a trace of Clarissa Harlowe's blood still flows in her veins: the "feminine aversion" to the alternative, rather than a specific interior process incorporated into the narrative, sends her to work making collars in a sweatshop. Thus Crane shows signs of relying on certain more traditional notions of character and methods of psychological representation than those which the story eventually develops, even as he begins to illustrate an environmental theory through his portrayal of Maggie's experience.

Premises and methods more distinctive and consistent with Crane's assumptions about the controlling force of circumstance begin to appear as Maggie's course, once plotted, swiftly unfolds. As her thoughts dwell increasingly on Pete, she becomes more aware of well-dressed women and the poverty of her own wardrobe, and more envious of "elegance and soft palms." Sensing that she is "gradually and surely shrivelling" in the stifling air and deadly routine of the shirt factory, she wonders "how long her youth would endure. She began to see the bloom upon her cheeks as valuable." Often the target of her mother's drunken wrath, she turns more and more to Pete, who "loomed like a golden sun" promising excitement, knowledge of a new and glamorous world, and escape from the vaguely discerned wretchedness of her present existence. The swaggering bartender eventually seduces her, an event we discover indirectly through a leering, noisome old woman who overhears and informs Jimmie of Maggie's tearful pleas for assurances of love from Pete. Cursed and disowned by her mother, whose usually inert moral sense is suddenly and hypocritically outraged, she goes to live with Pete and commits herself to his protection. At this point, as Maggie and Pete sit together in a cheap nightclub, Crane makes his most concentrated and extended effort to account for the movements of his heroine's mind:

> The sound of the music which, by the efforts of the frowsy-headed leader, drifted to her ears in the smoke-filled atmosphere, made the girl dream. She thought of her former Rum Alley environment and turned to regard Pete's strong protecting fists. She thought of a collar-and-cuff manufactory and the eternal moan of the proprietor: "What een hale do you sink I pie fife dolla a week for? Play? No, by tamn!" She contemplated Pete's man-subduing eyes and noted that wealth and prosperity were indicated by his clothes. She imagined a future rose-tinted because of its distance from all that she had experienced before.
>
> As to the present she perceived only vague reasons to be miserable. Her life was Pete's and she considered him worthy of the charge. She would be disturbed by no particular apprehensions so long as Pete adored her as he now said he did. She did not feel like a bad woman. To her knowledge she had never seen any better.[3]

Maggie's "dream" at this juncture is fundamentally different from her earlier musings on an ideal lover in a romantic dreamland. The connotations of "dim" in the earlier passage, now appear in the word "dream." Like strains of music and ribbons of smoke, which Crane imagines to be "drifting" and blending in the air, Maggie's thought drifts passively from past to future to present, settling in "vague" wreaths around problems which she understands only dimly and unanalytically. It is perhaps more accurate to say that her thought coils around her mental image of Pete, which is as central here as it was in the previous quotation. But whereas an abstract idealization of him constituted the whole of her idea in the previous passage as far as Crane's narrative focus was concerned, here an image made up of concrete details connoting physical "protection" and material security constitutes a mental indicator of her relation to the pressures of a threatening environment. The movement of Maggie's consciousness in search of or response to such indications is now the center of narrative interest.

Thus the "thought of her former . . . environment" triggers a self-reassuring glance at "Pete's strong protecting fists," which to her represent safety from her mother's blows and the predatory men of Rum Alley, even though Pete himself will soon tell her to "go to hell!" The thought of the shirt factory and its niggardly owner, whose "pocketbook [had] deprived [her] of the power of retort," prompts a comparable look (far from fully conscious "contemplation") at "Pete's man-subduing eyes," which are merely brazen but which signify to her the restoration of that power. Similarly, Pete's clothing, which is flashy rather than fine, indicates to her mind a vast improvement in "wealth and prosperity" over her sweatshop wages. The mental sum of these comparisons or indications, which are more like reflex actions than introspective analyses of her situation, is a blurry sense of the future as rose-tinted solely because her new environment is more comfortable than her old. Crane's environmentalism is more important here than the details of psychological processes which the theory implies, and the novelist looks no more closely at his heroine's imagined future. In this passage, however, he articulates his theory and its attendant ironies wholly by means of psychological narrative, whereas in the early scene he emphasized ironic contrasts at the expense of an explicitly psychological focus.

Maggie is no more self-conscious morally than she is introspectively aware of the real determinants of her choices and behavior. In an earlier sequence she and Pete attend a play in which, Crane tells us, "the dazzling heroine was rescued from the palatial home of her treacherous guardian by the hero with the beautiful sentiments." To Maggie "this was transcendental realism," and she "always departed with raised spirits from these melodramas. She rejoiced at how the poor and virtuous eventually overcame the wealthy and wicked. The theater made her think." [4] Clearly it made her think in conventional, moral categories, and regarding theatrical representation of a world completely removed from her own, Maggie's moral sense is keen—"She echoed the maledictions that the occupants of the gallery showered" on the villain, and with "untiring zeal [she] hissed vice and applauded virtue." She does not consciously abandon this moral sense in her own life; it simply does not enter in any fundamental way.

Thus, as the passage continues, her attempt at self-analysis is as vague as the smoke-like drift and dissolution of her thought in the first paragraph. "Reasons to be miserable" and "particular apprehensions" refer primarily to possibilities of change for the worse in her immediate environment, and only secondarily to her moral position as Pete's mistress. His adoration, which is actually something less sublime and which, in conventional terms, has already settled Maggie's moral hash, fends off such apprehensions and the need for *any* "particular" thinking on her part as long as it lasts. (Crane, however, represents this psychological fact in what James would call its "particular connexion" with the immediate situation.) Moral considerations enter only peripherally, and then only after the instinctual mechanics of accommodation with circumstance have finished operating. Although on the next page Maggie "with a shrinking movement, drew back her skirts" to avoid contact with a prostitute, an event which Crane relates without reference to her thoughts, this has little to do with the real basis of perception and action in the story, and serves merely as an ironic foreshadowing of Maggie's own effort to survive through prostitution after Pete loses interest in her. Here, Maggie "did not feel like a bad woman" after finding herself in a situation which is thoroughly bad by conventional standards, and did not think at all (at least not for the benefit of the narrative) of the moral implications beforehand. Environmental pressures rather than moral ones shape both her situation and her mental view of it. The reality which Crane posits, as distinct from the unreality of the melodrama he describes, allows for neither psychological nor dramatic alternatives in the course of Maggie's development.

Yet Crane, paradoxically and to the partial confusion of his deterministic theory, does not dispense altogether with a moral frame of reference in his portrayal of Maggie from this point on. In this regard it is interesting that he pays almost no direct attention to the workings of her mind through the remainder of the work, preferring to observe entirely from without her final humiliation by mother and brother, her rejection by Pete, and her movement toward "the blackness of the final block." When Pete shifts his attention to another woman, she "was dazed" and "could dimly perceive that something stupendous had happened." But this simply reinforces the established notion of her mind as vague and unreflective. She "asked aloud a question of herself: 'Who?' " after Pete slams the door on the threat she now embodies to his dubious respectability. But this figures in the narrative less as a mental process of Maggie's than as a rhetorical device of Crane's, signaling the final exhaustion of her options— "But where kin I go?" "Who" am I? She is not only without narrated thoughts on the rainy night that "a girl of the painted cohorts of the city" fails to find a customer and walks through the final block to the river; she is without even a name.

Jimmie, "arguing with himself, stumbling about in ways that he knew not" in an effort to reconcile his feelings about Maggie's ruin, "once, almost came to the conclusion that his sister would have been more firmly good had she better known how." He illustrates once more Crane's sense of the mind as dim and indistinct in its illumination and movement, and as possibly containing what James termed the "labyrinthine" complexities and Howells called the "fastnesses" of consciousness. Crane, however, attempts no direct analysis of such psychological recesses in this work, and Jimmie also "stumbles" toward Crane's most important conclusion about Maggie as the story moves toward its climax in her suicide. "Had she better known how"—had she grown up in easier circumstances, surrounded by nobler examples—Maggie would have acted in a different, and morally better, way. Jimmie, however, never reaches this conclusion. His own respectability seems to him to be in the balance, and he "threw . . . hastily aside" the idea that his sister is not responsible. Crane, of course, implies throughout the story that she is not, that environment has shaped her life regardless. To some slight extent, however, he seems to accept Jimmie's standards.

Crane, as well as a destructive environment, may thus be said to have a hand in Maggie's death. She drowns herself in despair, destroyed by the conditions of her existence, and innocent to the last in that these conditions make a sacrifice of her. But she also drowns herself because the "hell" to which Pete consigns her is in some small part a moral hell to which Crane, in spite of himself and regardless of extenuating environmental circumstances, allows her to be consigned. This is by no means the only reason for the relative absence of psychological scrutiny from the later portion of the novel—Crane's method throughout is geared to ironic juxtaposition or to the suggestion of an event through setting alone (as in the suicide scene), instead of to the "view from within" or even to the close study of mental events from without. Given his wavering at the conclusion between a moral attitude and an environmental theory, and given the almost wholly environmental fictive psychology in the main passage discussed, more continuous and intensive psychological representation as primary subject matter and unifying technique is virtually impossible for Crane in this work. No such uncertainty underlies *The Red Badge of Courage*. If uncertainty remains, it becomes part of the acknowledged psychological interest and accepted representational task of the novel. Here, in his masterpiece, Crane develops his concern with interior process to an almost Jamesian degree of fullness and "complication," and develops more flexible and various techniques through which to pursue his interest.

Crane's hero in *The Red Badge of Courage* is Henry Fleming, most often called "the youth," who, as the story opens, has enlisted in a New York regiment of the Union Army and has been sent to an unnamed front-line position. In earlier years Henry had dreamed of "Greeklike" battles, glorious and thrilling in their "sweep and fire," in which he imagined himself performing heroic feats. But he had also thought that "Greeklike struggle" had passed out of real life and over the horizon of the past. So he viewed the outbreak of the Civil War with "distrust," as if it "must be some sort of play affair." None the less, he had been eager to enlist; the war "might not be distinctly Homeric, but there seemed to be much glory in [it] . . . and he had longed to see it all." Indeed, his abstract sense of martial glory and his sense of heroism had been strengthened by the admiration and applause surrounding the regiment's departure. But the boredom of camp life, consisting in the winter months of little beyond "sitting still and trying to keep warm," had brought him back to a view of the war as a "vast blue demonstration," something essentially unreal in which his own part was neither heroic nor even significant. Such a mechanical exercise required only his physical presence, leaving his mind unengaged and free to speculate, in a recreational way, on the "thoughts which must agitate the minds of the generals."

Yet, at the beginning of the novel, when rumors of an impending battle spread through the camp, even though previous rumors had proven groundless, Henry finds himself wanting "to be alone with some new thoughts that had lately come to him":

> . . . There was a more serious problem. He lay in his bunk pondering upon it. He tried to mathematically prove to himself that he would not run from battle.
>
> Previously he had never felt obliged to wrestle too seriously with this question. In his life he had taken certain things for granted, never challenging his belief in ultimate success, and bothering little about means and roads. But here he was confronted with a thing of moment. It had suddenly appeared to him that perhaps in a battle he might run. He was forced to admit that as far as war was concerned he knew nothing of himself.
>
> A sufficient time before he would have allowed the problem to kick its heels at the outer portals of his mind, but now he felt compelled to give serious attention to it.
>
> A little panic-fear grew in his mind. As his imagination went forward to a fight, he saw hideous possibilities. He contemplated the lurking menaces of the future and failed in an effort to see himself standing stoutly in the midst of them. He recalled his visions of broken-bladed glory, but in the shadow of the impending tumult he suspected them to be impossible pictures.
>
> He sprang from the bunk and began to pace nervously to and fro. "Good Lord, what's th' matter with me?" he said aloud.
>
> He felt that in this crisis his laws of life were useless. Whatever he had learned of himself was here of no avail. He was an unknown quantity. He saw that he would again be obliged to experiment as he had in early youth. He must accumulate information of himself, and meanwhile he resolved to remain close upon his guard lest those qualities of which he knew nothing should everlastingly disgrace him. "Good Lord!" he repeated in dismay.[5]

This exposition of Henry's mental "problem" is not completely representative of Crane's fictive psychology in this novel, but it provides an important initial view of his assumptions about his hero's mind. The passage is important also because it suggests Crane's sense of the *literary* problem of psychological representation which he confronts in this work. The "thing of moment" here, psychologically speaking, is not merely Henry's abrupt awareness that he might in fact run, or his dismay when he suddenly realizes the irrelevance of "his laws of life," and consequently feels the need to experiment for a new kind of "information of himself." Of equal moment is Crane's interest in the processes by which such information is compiled and absorbed, and his own need to experiment with the methods by which he might trace its cumulative effect on Henry's mind. Just as Chad Newsome strikes Lambert Strether as "an absolutely *new* quantity" early in James's *The Ambassadors,* Henry Fleming is an "unknown quantity" psychologically to Crane at this point, as well as militarily to himself. His abstract and previously unchallenged "laws of life" (the phrase recalls the "law of mind" in *Uncle Tom's Cabin*) have melted into the mental "shadow" of inexperience and fear. In the crucible of war he will learn many things about himself and about the nature of reality. He will become known to the reader, however, primarily through Crane's increasingly concentrated observation of change in the quality of his perceptions, and of the relation between his interior processes and his behavior.

In this early passage, Crane is more concerned with the appearance of the problem in Henry's mind, with the gestation of what he calls Henry's "newborn question," than with directing the narrative toward a solution or answer. The youth's inability to grasp a solution, or even to comprehend fully the nature of the crisis by means of abstract "pondering" or mental "mathematics" is one of the novelist's basic points here. "Panic-fear" and "dismay," rather than measured "attention" or deliberate "contemplation," are the primary psychological facts of this sequence, even though certain aspects of the language seem at first to imply the opposite.

Phrases such as "obliged to wrestle," "forced to admit," "allowed the problem," "compelled to give serious attention," and "resolved to remain" suggest an introspective consciousness of a sort with which we are now quite familiar—a mind gifted with conscious control of its own movements, and more sensitive to values bearing on abstract questions than to the pressure of immediate circumstances. Even the setting—the bunk in which Henry "wished to be alone with some new thoughts"—reminds us of Isabel Archer's fireside armchair, or of the "close-curtained" mental retreats of certain other characters. Yet the importance of the mental processes to which these phrases refer is that they fail as conscious efforts to bring the problem under the control of conventional values which are taken for granted. The possibility that these processes are forced into motion in Henry's mind, without his conscious agency, by the pressure of unfamiliar circumstances is also an aspect of their narrative importance. It is as if the breakdown of his "laws of life," which previously were strong enough to keep the possibility of flight from battle safely beyond the "outer portals of his mind" and strong enough to withstand the intrinsic force of such an idea, had created a mental vacuum within those portals. By a kind of psychological implosion suggested in the piling up of passives ("felt obliged," "was confronted," "was forced," felt compelled," "be obliged"), the idea now rushes in to fill this void, moving at the same time to the center of Crane's narrative stage. The sequence of mental events becomes more closely identified with the sequence of the narrative itself.

Thus the "serious attention" which now occurs within the *inner* portals of Henry's mind amounts at least as much to an instinctive response to environmental change as it does to rational introspection. Crane's first reference to the quality of this attention is a reference to budding "panic-fear," which germinates deep within Henry's mind and grows toward full consciousness. Another image of organic mental process appears later in the story, when a "diamond-point of intelligence" gleams in the "glazed vacancy" of Henry's battle-stunned eyes and slowly intensifies into comprehension.[6] By contrast, in the fictive psychology of *Uncle Tom's Cabin* mental diamonds "sparkle suddenly," and even in the *Portrait* James represents another sort of panic-fear as a sudden flash of "white lightening." [7]

Henry's instinctive response to conditions under which his old "laws" or assumptions no longer pertain also pervades, simultaneously and of its own accord, his sense of both future and past. He does not consciously impel his imagination "forward to a fight"; it simply "went." Similarly, his recollection of past visions of imagined heroism is a panic-driven reflex from the failure of his conscious effort to believe in his future valor under fire. Like Strether, Henry does not think or ponder so much as "see" or "contemplate" in a purely visual sense. He perceives the pictures which his mind produces visually rather than analytically. The pictures of the future seem "hideously possible" in the absence of known laws for the environment of war; those from the past now seem "impossible" for the same reason. Both sorts of pictures, however—in the context of this scene as a thematic unit and in the context of the paragraph as a formal unit—spring directly from "panic-fear." The paragraph is also free of the passive constructions which dominate the first part of the passage, as if Crane could more easily consider the agency of mental process intrinsic to the mind itself once the narrative eye had passed (or imploded) through the "portals" of the mind, and begun to record the view from within.

Crane does not concentrate further on such a view in the present passage, but allows it to culminate in Henry's spoken question: "Good Lord, what's th' matter with me?" The question itself is nervously compulsive rather than calmly analytical (the boy has "sprung" up from the repose of his bunk), and accentuates the failure of introspective "mathematics" to resolve or even to clarify the problem at hand. Dismay, like blossoming fear or a brightening diamond-point of intelligence, has intensified to a climactic pitch in Henry's mind, in effect gathering all elements of uncertainty into a single, visceral query expressing the unknown quantity which it will be Crane's main purpose in the novel to examine and make known. The final paragraph is as much statement of this experimental purpose from Crane's point of view as it is a record of his hero's consciousness. The narrative lens moves back slightly from its subject; a mixture of general statements about Henry and specific reports about his thoughts replaces the concentrated analysis from within his mind which dominates the fourth and central paragraph; a passive construction reappears with its attendant vagueness as to psychological agency. Henry's conscious "resolve" also prepares for an ironic juxtaposition of the sort that occurs in *Maggie* at the expense of close scrutiny of the character's mind. Shortly, he will run from the battle. His mental "guard" proves irrelevant to the unknown qualities within him when confronted by the previously unexperienced forces around him, which combine to produce this act. His "resolve" is worthless against these qualities and forces. In *The Red Badge,* however, Crane's irony takes effect through his close examination of Henry's interior reactions, through his "experimental" measuring of the closing distance between Henry's useless preconceptions of life and the reality from which his new "laws" must be drawn.

Once again like Lambert Strether, Henry has found that "there was no computing" by an old calculus for newer and more accurate "information of himself." For several days after his experience in the passage discussed,

> he made ceaseless calculations, but they were all wondrously unsatisfactory. He found that he could establish nothing. . . . He reluctantly admitted that he could not sit still and with a mental slate and pencil derive an answer. To gain it, he must have blaze, blood, and danger, even as a chemist requires this, that and the other.[8]

Crane now proceeds to gather and combine the necessary "chemical" ingredients for his own literary experiment, to expose Henry with a vengeance to what James would later call (with less violent contrasts in mind) "the action of another air," and he begins to set down in narrative form the psychological results.

Finally, when the battle breaks out, the entire regiment undergoes a "sudden change from the ponderous infantry of theory to the light and speedy infantry of practice." Something similar begins to occur in the movements of Henry's mind when he is first exposed to "blaze, blood, and danger," though neither his theory of the war as a meaningless demonstration nor his abstract vision of glory and terror immediately vanish. At one point, during the process of moving into position with the rest of his regiment, all his "ceaseless calculations" about how he might prevent himself from running harden into a single, specific "calculating" look about him to estimate the chance of escape before the battle is even joined. No narrated process precedes this momentary calculation, no use is made of the mental slate and pencil. It is simply an instinctive mental thrust of which he is hardly aware. And although Crane reports the internal event with complete omniscience, his use of the active voice creates some sense of dramatic immediacy. Soon after, in sight of the advancing enemy and unable to make his "faltering intellect" recall even having loaded his gun, he "instantly ceased to debate the question" upon casting a single, specific glance at the onrushing foe: "Before he was ready to begin—before he had announced to himself that he was about to fight—he threw the obedient, well-balanced rifle into position and fired." Crane repeatedly emphasizes the disorientation which causes Henry's mind to "fly in all directions": the jolted perceptions of these early moments in battle "were never perfect to him afterward, but remained a mass of blurred shapes." Yet, here at the start his mechanical response to the requirements of the situation is perfectly "well-balanced" to mental commands which have little to do with his rational intellect.

Henry, nevertheless, thinks in abstractions, insofar as he still manages to think continuously in the growing confusion. He "expected a battle scene" patterned after his visions of "Greeklike" conflict, despite the actuality of the battle unfolding before his eyes. He "expected to see the stealthy approach of his death" somehow personified, instead of perceiving an immediate, concrete threat to his life. Crane sums up the abstract expectations, bred in his hero's mind by inexperience and fear, with a personification approaching mythic proportions, locating it quite near to Henry's mental projections if not actually reporting it from within such a process: "They were going to look at war, the red animal—war, the blood-swollen god." At the same time, the youth is receiving a great many more immediate impressions—"A thousand details of color and form surged in his mind"—but as yet Crane neither specifies and describes these details, nor incorporates their surge into the basic thrust of his narrative.

Thus, when Henry turns and runs, the horror presumably inspiring this act lies not in the concrete predicament but in "those things which he imagined," none of which Crane specifies beyond having previously shown certain of Henry's abstract imaginings. He is well on his way, turned from the battle, before *we* see that horror reflected in his face. Of his actual "decision" to flee—a mechanical reaction to animal instinct—Crane tells us only the following in the calm language of the scientific observer, and before telling us anything else:

> For a moment, in the great clamor, he was like a proverbial chicken. He lost the direction of safety. Destruction threatened him from all points.
>
> Directly he began to speed . . .[9]

Henry's first conscious reaction to his flight is an extended attempt to rationalize it in terms of a highly moral theory of self-preservation, a theory which he himself puts to a kind of experimental test. The bewildered dartings of a "proverbial chicken" become, in this sequence of thought, "sagacious" escape from annihilation, the cardinal among a set of "very correct and commendable rules." The bearings he completely lost in the actual situation return as a convicition that "intelligent deliberation"—computation by mental slate and pencil—will prove his sagacity and the folly of those who remained in position. Henry proves this rationalization to his own temporary satisfaction by tossing a pine cone at a squirrel which promptly scampers away in "chattering fear":

> There was the law, he said. Nature had given him a sign.[10]

His mind has been much occupied with erecting new theories and laws either to vindicate or to replace his old ones, since his initial consciousness of breakdown in the laws of life.

Beneath this stratum of rationalization, however, flows a current of less patterned and more immediate impressions. Even though "he told himself" that his course had been the correct one, his "mind *heard* [italics mine] howls of derision" from imagined comrades. Even though he consciously considers that his motives were "righteous," he instinctively cringes before a vague guilt for which even his superior wisdom "can find no words." While he thinks that Nature has granted him an absolving sign, he projects his guilt and fear of being discovered onto the clutching branches of surrounding trees and feels that he cannot "conciliate" the forest. As the winding passageway through which Strether approaches Gloriani's garden in *The Ambassadors* refers in part to his intricate maneuverings in unfamiliar psychological terrain, so Henry's "wendings" through the woods in search of "dark and intricate places" refer in part to his involuntary entry, bereft of habitual bearings, into the labyrinth of his own mind.[11] Here, very slowly, he will begin to accumulate new "information of himself."

On the literal level, Henry wends his way toward the forest "chapel" in which he finds the ant-infested corpse. Here, the thousand details of color and form surging in his mind, which have not yet been translated into dramatic texture and narrative motion, cohere into an image commanding extended narrative attention. Henry sees, and feels himself to be seen by, the horror he had earlier envisioned abstractly, now invested with horrifically concrete color and form. His mind is indeed, in the literal sense of impressions assaulting it, "horror-stricken." What he sees we see, although technically speaking not through his mind but through Crane's arrangement of visual detail. The corpse is an ineradicable fact, real, "a thing." Yet it is also a vision encountered in the depths of the mental labyrinth, a primary interior recognition, however unconscious or momentary, of a reality so far unacknowledged and therefore unknown. The "subtle suggestion" Henry receives to touch the dead man, and the feeling that he himself is deadened, "for moments turned to stone" while exchanging a look with him, confirm this sense of interior communion. The entire scene—and in this case the dramatic and visual senses of the term are fused—confirms the increasing importance in Crane's fictive psychology of the relation between minutely perceived external reality and thematic concern with internal change.

Here Crane does more than merely buttress an environmental theory, as he does in *Maggie,* by depicting a character's mental processes as instinctual and mechanical. In *The Red Badge* the pervasive animal and mechanical images dramatize his theory without restricting Henry's mental movement to the passive mechanism that characterizes Maggie's mind. But the importantly new idea in this sequence is a sense of Crane's interest in a process of discovery which was impossible for Maggie, given the simplicity of her mental mechanics and the dimness of her inward vision. In the earlier work, Crane's environmentalism precluded and so rendered representationally and thematically irrelevant clearer inward sight on his heroine's part. Here, however, as in *The Ambassadors,* a sharply perceived aspect of reality and the inwardly visual process through which that perception is achieved have become one and the same: thematic end and representational means. The reality suggested by the corpse, like that suggested by Strether's image of life as an inescapable tin mold into which the helpless jelly of consciousness is poured, is deterministic. What Joseph Conrad was to call "the moral problem of conduct," however, remains an issue for Crane in *The Red Badge,* as it does for James in *The Ambassadors.* "Seeing" clearly is for both authors prerequisite to the solution of this problem, and perhaps the most important element of narrative "conduct" itself, even though the actual process of vision is environmentally determined.

In this context this process is now firmly established as the basis of narrative development in *The Red Badge.* Crane's omniscience is in a way our own, since he uses it to amplify and not to restrict our sense of what goes on in the character's mind, whether or not he attempts a continuous dramatization of mental activity strictly from within. After Henry's confrontation with the corpse, Crane makes a statement about him suggesting the existence in this novel of what James called in the "Preface to *The Portrait of a Lady*" a "general plan" of psychological representation:

> His accumulated thought . . . was used to form scenes. The noise was as the voice of an eloquent being, describing.[12]

The remark is a light and speedy reference to a particular situation rather than a ponderous theory of the mind in fiction, and is therefore neither attached to nor "supremely illustrated" by an extended passage such as the vigil chapter of the *Portrait.* In a convincing if not in a technically strict sense, however, this notion is borne out by the rest of the novel.

Hence the enigmatic clarity of the famous "wafer" image of the sun at the end of the grotesquely "rite-like" episode of Jim Conklin's death. Visually distinct, conceptually rich and perplexing, the image "accumulates" for the reader into a momentary "scene"—a moment of Henry's seeing—of the spellbound awe and livid rage he feels when he watches Conklin die. Beyond this, it may carry all or some or none of the various ironic meanings which critics have attached to it. The *perceptual* importance of Henry's charged vision of the sun is similar to that of his encounter with the corpse in the forest. The sun, like the corpse, simply is; it concentrates visually a flat, implacable reality in which conventional "concilia-tions" or "philippics" are irrelevant. The sight of the sun abruptly cuts off Henry's futile curse against fate and war in the abstract, and makes him "throw aside his mental pamphlets on the philoso-phy of the retreated and rules for the guidance of the damned."

The youth eventually rejoins his regiment, suffering agonies of fear of exposure and guilt, yet accepting the measure of recogni-tion that his wound—a red badge of nascent courage as well as the ironic emblem of his shame—creates for him among his fellows. When he awakens from exhausted sleep, for a moment imagining himself in a charnel house, he achieves along with his "proper mind" a clearer perception of the "facts of the present" in relation to visions of the past or prophecies of the future than he has yet possessed. In noting the transformation of the "loud soldier," he senses his own development of "new eyes." When next he goes into battle, he feels that he has entered "a clearer atmosphere":

> There was an effect like a revelation in the new appearance of the landscape. . . .
>
> It seemed to the youth that he saw everything. Each blade of green grass was bold and clear. He thought that he was aware of every change in the thin, transparent vapor that floated idly in sheets. The brown or gray trunks of the trees showed each roughness of their surfaces. And the men of the regiment, with their starting eyes and sweating faces, running madly, or falling, as if thrown headlong, to queer, heaped-up corpses—all were comprehended. His mind took a mechanical but firm impression, so that afterward every-

> thing was pictured and explained to him, save why he himself was there.[13]

The "mass of blurred shapes" which had been Henry's first impressions of war have become crystalline images constituting a mental scene. Details of color and form still "surge" in his consciousness, but as if in slow motion, allowing each sensory nuance to reach its perfection. From a lens fitted with filters admitting only certain aspects of reality and distorting others, his mind has developed into a photographic plate reacting to "everything," a mechanism that "comprehends" only in the sense of passively taking in, and which "explains" only in the sense of reproducing in pictorial form the data it records. Henry saw everything, and *what* he saw "accounts for everything," to repeat James's phrase in the preface to *The Ambassadors.* The "why" of things, however, lies beyond its function or control.

This passage marks the completion of Henry's psychological adaptation to a changed environment, and of a shift in Crane's determinism from a concept of undefined exterior force exhibited in *Maggie* to one of minutely observed (if not directly dramatized) interior mechanics developed in *The Red Badge.* Yet the "why" of things, and indeed to a considerable extent "the moral problem of conduct," remain unsolved issues in this novel. Crane's explanation of Henry's failure to consider consciously "why he himself was there," distinct and set apart textually from the photographic "explanation" of the scene itself, is given in language suggesting moral rather than physical or purely mechanical courage:

> There was a delirium that encounters despair and death, and is heedless and blind to the odds. It is a temporary but sublime absence of selfishness.[14]

Crane admits this explanation even though, a few pages later, he describes the heedless rush of the regiment's charge as physiologically based, the result of "exhilarating fluid" in their systems. The shift in tense from "there was" to "there is," moreover, implies a shift from direct, concretely descriptive concern with the scene just etched on Henry's mind, to more general concern with abstractly expoundable psychological law. Crane has gradually shown the real laws of Henry's life to be enforced through mechanical, perhaps even biochemical processes, rather than through moral tradition or ideals of sublimely heroic action. He hints here, however, at something "sublime" in an action supposedly based in automatic response. Abstract values or laws seem not to have ceased altogether to operate in the world of the novel.

The author's concluding observations of his hero's mind elaborate upon, without fully clarifying, this mixture of moral and psychological concern. The battle is over, and a transformative era in Henry's experience is completed. Crane attempts to summarize the meaning of that experience through an account of the character's own effort at mental review:

> For a time the youth was obliged to reflect in a puzzled and uncertain way. His mind was undergoing a subtle change. It took moments for it to cast off its battleful ways and resume its accustomed course of thought. Gradually his brain emerged from the clogged clouds, and at last he was enabled to more closely comprehend himself and circumstance. . . .
>
> Later he began to study his deeds, his failures, and his achievements. Thus, fresh from the scenes where many of his usual machines of reflection had been idle, from where he had proceeded sheeplike, he struggled to marshal all his acts.
>
> At last they marched before him clearly. From this present view-point he was enabled to look upon them in spectator fashion and to criticise them with some correctness, for his new condition had already defeated certain sympathies.
>
> Regarding his procession of memory he felt gleeful and unregretting, for in it his public deeds were paraded in great

> and shining prominence. Those performances which had been witnessed by his fellows marched now in wide purple and gold, having various deflections. They went gayly with music. It was pleasure to watch these things. He spent delightful minutes viewing the gilded images of memory.
>
> He saw that he was good. . . .
>
> Nevertheless, the ghost of his flight from the first engagement appeared to him and danced. There were small shoutings in his brain about these matters. For a moment he blushed, and the light of his soul flickered with shame. . . .
>
> Yet gradually he mustered force to put the sin at a distance. And at last his eyes seemed to open to some new ways.[15]

The "subtle change" in Henry's interior processes in which Crane is persistently interested throughout the novel has already occurred. It culminated in the cinematic lucidity of the youth's perceptions during the recent engagement (as distinct from the still lucidity of Isabel's retrospections during her vigil). In some respects this final change is a return to his original condition, as well as a device through which to comment on a new condition.

Here, as in the passage about the latest skirmish, Crane uses the accumulated thought of his hero to create narrative scenes. Now, however, the scenes are formally arranged, consciously introspective, and subject to moral interpretation. The moral problem, which was the object of Henry's anticipatory "figurings" and "diagrams" with mental slate and pencil, is also the object of his conscious "struggle to marshal all his acts" in retrospective procession. His mental processes are still mechanical operations, but now they are once again "his usual machines of reflection," machines which resume a conscious and customary course of thought instead of becoming permanently adapted to new tasks. His brain, as a perceptual mechanism, was actually at its most precise shortly before this passage, and is now, to some extent, returning into abstract "clouds" or imagined heroism in the "gilded images of memory." Despite the small moral shoutings in this brain, the flickering light of shame in his "soul" bears the main burden of representing Henry's guilty memory.

The experience of war brings Henry "to more closely comprehend [in the intellectual, as well as the technical sense] himself and circumstance," to understand something of the environmental forces which have been exerted on him through the medium of his mind. Some readers disagree, insisting that Crane's irony is total to the last, and that the "sympathies" which Henry's experience has defeated are the very qualities which might truly have enlarged his awareness of reality, and corrected his view of himself. This interpretation perhaps lends consistency to the mechanistic aspect of Crane's fictive psychology, but I find it an oversimplification of the very sort it attacks: the notion that Crane offers a neat and wholly satisfactory solution to Henry's moral problem, and that psychological grounds for this solution are relatively unimportant. What Henry achieves here is not the "moral vindication" which he sought while trying to rationalize desertion, but the "force" of character—and in a more literal sense the mechanical force of mind—to absorb the knowledge of his sin and go on. He "puts the sin at a distance," but does not omit it from the information he has gained about himself. The abstractly moral and concretely psychological aspects of Crane's concern, therefore, remain in somewhat uneasy balance, as the archaic elements in the technique of this passage imply. But here these aspects of Crane's concern are considerably less sharply opposed to or distinct from one another than in *Maggie*. In different terms from those we have seen developed in the works of James and Howells, the movement of a character's mind has become the medium within which a particular moral problem may be explored, rather than remaining a secondary element of fiction through which a general set of moral values—or an environmental theory—may be illustrated and enforced.

It nevertheless remains for Frank Norris, and to a greater extent Theodore Dreiser, writers whose careers are being launched as

Crane's is abruptly ending, to confront the problem of balance between the psychological and the moral aspects of the novelist's concern. By looking at these interests as essentially one, they complete the "experiment" in fictive psychology undertaken by Crane, and construct their moral meanings entirely in terms of its results.

FIVE

The Voice of Want: Frank Norris and Theodore Dreiser

The clock of thought ticks out its wish . . .

Sister Carrie

Norris's *McTeague* (1899) and Dreiser's *Sister Carrie* (1900) bear a different relation to one another than do the works already examined. Perhaps this relation most nearly reflects, and in a sense repeats in an altered form, the pattern of the chapter which focused on James's *Watch and Ward* and Howells's *A Chance Acquaintance*. In that chapter, we observed in essentially contemporary novels by essentially contemporary writers, each of whom was just embarking on a long and distinguished career, closely related (if potentially distinct) stirrings in fictive psychology against a background of established convention. Here, in novels published just a year apart by writers almost the same age, both beginning important if not uniformly long and distinguished careers, we shall be concerned with psychological portrayals which seem in some sense (if not in the sense of linear historical change) to be rooted in those early stirrings.

It is obvious that neither the gradual, consistent evolution of James's psychological mastery over a period of nearly thirty years, nor the less evenly shifting basis of Howells's psychological interest during the critical decade of the 1880's, nor even the sudden surge of interior color and form in Crane's work, brings us to the point represented in the Introduction by Dreiser's discussion of Hurstwood's decline. This chapter is more concerned with exploring complementary relations between novels than with tracing developmental relations among them over time. *Uncle Tom's Cabin* provided a necessary background to the discussion of *Watch and Ward* and *A Chance Acquaintance,* enabling us to see both common roots and diverse capacities for growth in fictive psychology around 1870. Now, *McTeague* provides another sort of comparative context for our discussion of *Sister Carrie,* helping us to see both shared conceptual soil and diversified representational outgrowths in fictive psychology around 1900.

In *McTeague,* Norris depicts the degeneration and death of a huge, ox-strong, slow-witted man from the California mining country, who has become a passably competent but unlicensed dentist in San Francisco. "McTeague's mind was as his body, heavy, slow to act, sluggish." Yet in a rudimentary way McTeague is observant —he never tires of watching the panorama of life on the street below his cramped office-apartment, ceaselessly changing and recurring with the time of the day and the day of the week. His life has a primitive regularity, sensual but controlled, consisting of work on weekdays and on Sundays of a heavy noon meal followed by a drowsy smoke and "gorged" sleep. His father had been a shift-boss in a Placer County mine, steady for thirteen out of fourteen days, and on alternate Sundays "an irresponsible animal, a beast, a brute, crazy with alcohol." McTeague's Sunday ritual reflects his improved, if still somewhat tenuous control over brute needs and instincts in his own nature.

Early in the story McTeague meets Trina Sieppe, a middle-class girl of ordinary charm brought to him for repair of a broken tooth by her cousin Marcus Schouler, with whom the dentist is friendly and with whom the girl is keeping company. The dental work requires several sittings, and McTeague gradually becomes acquainted, and then preoccupied, with the first girl he has ever permitted to enter his consciousness:

> Trina was McTeague's first experience. With her the feminine element suddenly entered his little world. It was not only her that he saw and felt, it was the woman, the whole sex, an entire new humanity, strange and alluring, that he seemed to have discovered. How had he ignored it so long? It was dazzling, delicious, charming beyond all words. His narrow point of view was at once enlarged and confused. . . . Everything had to be made over again. His whole rude idea of life had to be changed. The male virile desire in him tardily awakened, aroused itself, strong and brutal. It was resistless, untrained, a thing not to be held in leash an instant.[1]

In *The Ambassadors* the unsuspected light suffusing a new medium of experience "dazzles" Strether's inward eye. In *The Red Badge of Courage* comprehension begins as a "diamond point of intelligence," a "dazzle," imprinted on the photographic plate of Henry's mind. Here, in *McTeague,* although with much less representational concreteness and precision, a new element in the character's environment and experience makes an impact on his mind, confusing—"dazzling"—and expanding the range of its habitual processes. The categories within which Strether's initial assumptions about life are arranged, although far from "rude," shatter under the assault of the vivid facts of a larger reality, just as Henry Fleming's "laws of life" are subverted by exposure to the action of another air. McTeague's "whole rude idea of life [has now] to be changed" as well, in the light of this newly discovered dimension to reality.

Norris's abstract conception of this dimension, "the feminine element," Woman with her "strange allure," is found similarly stated in fiction of a much earlier date. Indeed, Lawrence's discovery of Nora's suddenly ripening womanhood in *Watch and Ward,* and Roderick's reaction to Christina's spell in *Roderick Hudson,* are rendered by James in similarly abstract terms. But the change in McTeague which Norris is most concerned with representing here (itself an abstractly conceived element of masculine type rather than a dramatized process), seems unlikely to refine, however drastically it may alter, McTeague's rude idea of life: "male virile desire, . . . strong and brutal." Sexuality as complicated interior process, distinguished from sex as simplified conventional type (the innocent heroine, the temptress, the morally wise wife), has gone almost unacknowledged in fictive psychology thus far surveyed. Although implicit in the key relationships of *Roderick* and *A Modern Instance,* although a latent factor in Isabel's relation to Goodwood in the *Portrait,* and although more specifically implied if not analytically treated in *Maggie,* sexuality never really emerges in the work of James or Howells or Crane as a subject of intrinsic psychological interest, as an aspect of real experience requiring (or allowed) careful psychological scrutiny.

To Norris, however, lurking centrally within what James called "the labyrinth," Howells termed "those fastnesses," Crane considered the inner "portals," and Norris himself calls "the black, unsearched penetralia" of the mind, is the "mystery of sex." [2] He finds the mystery "strange" as well as calling it so from McTeague's point of view in this passage, just as every other writer with whom we have dealt has at some point found interior process "strange" and difficult to represent. His portrayal of its workings in this novel is as dependent on the popular Darwinism he learned from LeConte while a student at Berkeley as James's and Howells's portrayals of their earliest heroines' minds are dependent on the essentially Christian (if by then fully secularized) conventions of innocence. Yet as Larzer Ziff observes in *The American 1890's: Life and Times of a Lost Generation:*

> Norris was the full beneficiary of both the literary merits and literary vices that were consequences of popular Darwinism. If his uncritical acceptance of it finally kept him from being a great writer, the genius which was released, once this handle to the world was grasped, brought into American literature not only a new cast of characters but a closer observation and shrewder delineation of the problems they shared with their fellows—not the least of which was sexuality.[3]

Sexuality is by no means the sole or even the central concern of American novelists at the close of our period; it is, however, a shared element in the fictive psychologies of the works with which we now conclude our discussion. It is more clearly acknowledged as psychological fact in these novels than in earlier works, and is therefore admitted to more intensive representation in psychological terms. Its varying treatments help to illustrate the new "geography" (to borrow James's term from *The Ambassadors*) of fictive psychology broadly viewed at the century's end. If this geography is in some respects as restricted as the old, if its contours conform to assumptions about the mind and the nature of reality which are as abstract as those in the early works of James or Howells, it is nevertheless fundamentally changed from that which we observed at the outset.

Reaching a stage in his work on Trina's tooth which is particularly painful to her, McTeague places her under an anaesthetic:

> He put the sponge a half-dozen times to Trina's face, more nervous than he had ever been before, watching the symptoms closely. Her breathing became short and irregular;

there was a slight twitching of the muscles. When her thumbs turned inward toward the palms, he took the sponge away. She passed off very quickly, and, with a long sigh, sank back into the chair.

. . . For some time he stood watching her as she lay there, unconscious and helpless, and very pretty. He was alone with her, and she was absolutely without defence.

Suddenly the animal in the man stirred and woke; the evil instincts that in him were so close to the surface leaped to life, shouting and clamouring.

It was a crisis—a crisis that had arisen all in an instant; a crisis for which he was totally unprepared. Blindly, and without knowing why, McTeague fought against it, moved by an unreasoned instinct of resistance. Within him, a certain second self, another better McTeague rose with the brute; both were strong, with the huge crude strength of the man himself. The two were at grapples. There in that cheap and shabby "Dental Parlour" a dreaded struggle began. It was the old battle, old as the world, wide as the world—the sudden panther leap of the animal, lips drawn, fangs aflash, hideous, monstrous, not to be resisted, and the simultaneous arousing of the other man, the better self that cries, "Down, down," without knowing why; that grips the monster; that fights to strangle it, to thrust it down and back.

Dizzied and bewildered by the shock, the like of which he had never known before, McTeague turned from Trina, gazing bewilderedly about the room. The struggle was bitter; his teeth ground themselves together with a little rasping sound; the blood sang in his ears; his face flushed scarlet; his hands twisted themselves together like the knotting of cables. . . . But for all that he shook his huge head from time to time, muttering:

"No, by God! No, by God!" . . .

He turned to his work, as if seeking a refuge in it. But as he drew near to her again, the charm of her innocence and helplessness came over him afresh. It was a final protest against his resolution. Suddenly he leaned over and kissed

> her, grossly, full on the mouth. The thing was done before he knew it.[4]

In this passage, and throughout the novel, Norris purports to be "watching the symptoms" of interior change in McTeague as closely as the dentist observes the physiological effects of the anaesthetic on his patient. McTeague's mind is Norris's subject here in somewhat the same sense that Trina is McTeague's patient. The narrative lens, rather than being placed within McTeague's consciousness or being used to project events directly from his mind, is ostensibly diagnostic, a point from which the author may detachedly observe empirically verifiable occurrences within a subject who is under prolonged literary study and treatment.

The narrator, however, as well as the character, is under influences which interfere with his objective attention to the immediate, directly observable situation. In *A Modern Instance,* Howells theorized the existence of a "sense of prey" within even the most conventionally romantic "transports" of a man in love. He neither imagined this sense in explicitly sexual terms nor pursued the concept into more concrete representational form, and it remained only tentatively associated with the actual movements of Bartley's mind, despite its relevance to the overall meaning. Here, a sense of prey asserts itself in McTeague, and takes a definite place in the mental narrative as soon as he realizes Trina's defenselessness. It *is* explicitly sexual, and it is *itself* the transport of feeling which initially erupts within him, "shouting and clamouring." Whereas Henry Fleming experienced "small shoutings in his brain" while reflecting on his instinctive desertion, the shouting in McTeague's brain is the suddenly dominant voice of instinct itself, preceding and precluding reflection of any kind. Nevertheless, from the point at which the interior battle is joined between "the animal" in McTeague and his "other, better" self (the former taking textual precedence throughout this sequence), Norris's psychological narrative shifts away from the immediately dramatic toward the theoretical and even the allegorical. While particular shoutings and clamorings await representation in the externally observed symptoms of the fifth paragraph, the longer and central fourth paragraph abstracts the struggle into a LeContean tableau, an emblematic "daguerreotype" quite differently conceived and composed but no less cosmic in scope than those controlling psychological representation in *Uncle Tom's Cabin.*

Just as Silas Lapham's "selfish" interests and Basil March's "abject" impulses bear the full moral weight of Howells's adjectives only when they run out of rational control, McTeague's "evil instincts"—his brute sensuality—is evil only because it is out of such control. Similarly, his equally "unreasoned instinct of resistance" is a movement toward, if not itself a rational act of, control over the brute, rather than a movement toward moral right. Moral awareness, the "knowledge of why," is no more important here in a situation of blind instinctual conflict than it is to the photographic clarity of Henry's climactic perceptions of war in *The Red Badge.* A system of values having to do with a proper state of balanced interaction between (to quote LeConte) "the more robust lower . . . [and] the diviner higher" [5] aspects of human nature, along with a concept of primal opposition between these aspects in mankind generally rather than in McTeague specifically, is Norris's real subject in this paragraph. A static, enlarged image of "the old battle, old as the world, wide as the world" supersedes for the moment continued narration of the present battle in McTeague's Dental Parlor. An image of the primal panther frozen in mid-leap and the man arrested in his movement to meet it superimposes itself on the actual psychic shock of their collision in McTeague, thus freezing for the moment the narrative reverberations of that shock.

The stream of immediate mental events flows around this central paragraph, which in turn determines its flow to a degree but which remains an emblem of Norris's theory of internal process, and not a dramatization of psychological fact. Norris returns to the precise physiological observations with which he began the sequence, and to the development "in the particular connexion" of the sense of prey which eventually determines McTeague's act. This process in McTeague is distinct from the archetypal impasse —statically expressed and resulting in no specific action—between preying and resisting instincts in all men. McTeague himself is no match for the animal within him; his sensuality lies "close to the surface," and nothing in our specific knowledge of him up to this point leads us to expect an equal struggle. Just as the "Holy Spirit indwelling" fails to account in *A Hazard of New Fortunes* for interior changes which it accounts for entirely in *Uncle Tom's Cabin;* just as Henry's conscious "resolve" in *The Red Badge of Courage* melts before the animal impulse toward safety in spite of his conventional appeal to the "Good Lord"; so McTeague's "resolution" and his muttered "No, by God!" (by this time totally removed from any literal apprehension of a divine reality) are irrelevant to his action. Trina's "innocence," rather than appealing to his higher nature and "charming" his lower into harmlessness as Nora's innocence charms Fenton in *Watch and Ward,* simply arouses the beast to its decisive leap.

Fictive psychology in *McTeague* thus remains divided in a sense not previously encountered in our study. Norris writes about a process which is physiologically determined, unconsciously experienced by the character, and detachedly observed by the author. It is important to narrative as action rather than as awareness, a matter of what happens or is done rather than of what is seen or known. Yet the force he imagines as driving the process, the scheme he imagines as controlling its operation, is an abstract conception removed from the action and from the passage of time, and positing a moral consciousness or a moral instinct to struggle with purely physical urges. Norris allegorizes this conception at greater length than he dramatizes the process, and he does so in language more charged morally than that prevailing elsewhere in the passage (despite an excess of melodramatic verbiage throughout). The power of primal conflict, "old as the world," over the present movements of McTeague's brain, and over their representation by the author, is similar in its effect—though diametrically opposed in its essence—to the power of scripture "through all time" over the narrative movements of Uncle Tom's soul.

In the opening sentence of Chapter 10 in *Sister Carrie,* after Carrie has become Drouet's mistress and is established in a comfortable apartment, Dreiser writes: "In the light of the world's attitude toward woman and her duties, the nature of Carrie's mental state deserves consideration." In James's *Watch and Ward,* the novelist basically accepts the world's attitude toward woman and her duties as his own, and the mental state of his heroine neither requires nor receives much attention as he works out her performance of that role and those duties to their conventional conclusion. Here, precisely because a conventional attitude no longer suffices for the novelist to account for his heroine's actions, careful consideration of the processes underlying those actions becomes his primary thematic concern and representational resource.

In the eyes of the world, Carrie has simply fallen; in Dreiser's view she has acted in response to real forces, both within and without herself, that the world has not yet learned to recognize. His immediate task is to account for her situation in terms of these forces, to lay a foundation for the continuation of narrative beyond this point by indicating the nature of the relation between psychological and environmental realities as he conceives them. His longer-range concern, based and dependent on his handling of the immediate representational problem, is considerably broader:

> For all the liberal analysis of Spencer and our modern naturalistic philosophers, we have but an infantile perception of morals. There is more in the subject than mere conformity to the law of evolution. It is yet deeper than conformity to things of earth alone. It is more involved than we, as yet,

> perceive. Answer first, why the heart thrills [and how the mind works—emotion and desire are integral to psychological process in Dreiser's view]. . . . In the essence of these facts lie the first principles of morals.[6]

Dreiser might have said "for all . . . our modern naturalistic" *novelists* as well, for to him there is much more in the subject than conformity such as McTeague's to the evolutionary principle posited by Norris, though this does not mean that Dreiser rejects that principle, or one very much like it in certain ways. The point is that although "the heart thrills" in fiction of all periods, novelists according to Dreiser have not yet properly inquired as to "why"—and still more importantly as to *how*—it does so. Morality, however—basic attitudes toward problems of value and meaning in life and therefore in art—must be approached through careful consideration of the psychological "facts," consideration more "liberally analytical" than Dreiser thinks philosophers *or* novelists have yet achieved.

He now turns to this problem in what James would call its "particular connexion" with his heroine's immediate situation:

> Here, then, was Carrie, established in a pleasant fashion, free of certain difficulties which most ominously confronted her, laden with many new ones which were of a mental order, and altogether so turned about in all her earthly relationships that she might well have been a new and different individual. She looked into her glass and saw a prettier Carrie than she had seen before; she looked into her mind, a mirror prepared of her own and the world's opinions, and saw a worse. Between these two images she wavered, hesitating which to believe.
>
> "My, but you're a little beauty," Drouet was wont to exclaim to her.
>
> She would look at him with large, pleased eyes. . . .
>
> Her conscience, however, was not a Drouet, interested in

> praise. There she heard a different voice, with which she argued, pleaded, excused. It was no just and sapient counsellor, in its last analysis. It was only an average little conscience, a thing which represented the world, her past environment, habit, convention, in a confused way. With it, the voice of the people was truly the voice of God.
>
> "Oh, thou failure!" said the voice.
>
> "Why?" she questioned.
>
> "Look at those about you," came the whispered answer. "Look at those who are good. How they would scorn to do what you have done. Look at the good girls; how will they draw away from such as you when they know you have been weak. You had not tried before you failed.
>
> It was when Carrie was alone, looking out across the park, that she would be listening to this. It would come infrequently—when something else did not interfere, when the pleasant side was not too apparent, when Drouet was not there. It was something clear in utterance at first, but never wholly convincing. There was always an answer, always the December days threatened. She was alone; she was desireful; she was fearful of the whistling wind. The voice of want made answer for her.[7]

In Carrie as in Maggie, problems of a consciously "mental order" arise only in the wake of essentially instinctive responses to and accommodations with environmental stimuli and circumstances. Carrie has resolved certain quite practical, immediately "ominous" difficulties—problems of food, heat, clothing, perhaps of sexual gratification as well—by accepting Drouet's arrangement. Unlike Maggie, however, who feels "no particular apprehension" of a moral nature so long as the improvement of her physical environment gained through Pete's attentions lasts, Carrie experiences moral confusion, if not apprehension, upon finding herself "turned about" in her relations to the world. Like many characters already discussed she feels new and different. Dreiser's implied question as far as his narrative treatment of this change is concerned is how it has operated, and why it has resulted in the present situation.

Looking at her mirror, which reflects physical reality just as the photographic plate of Henry's mind records it in *The Red Badge of Courage,* Carrie sees not only a prettier self, but in the environmental sense of the word a better self. This is her first perception, just as the act of accepting Drouet precedes her reflection upon it. Looking by a conscious act of moral introspection "into her mind," which Dreiser at this point represents as simple conscience, a mirror of conventional values, she sees the worse self she has become in the opinion of society. Dreiser suggests the difference between the view from within and the view from without, both of which have a place in his fictive psychology, rather than committing himself (as does James) to direct representation of the former without acknowledging the latter. What Carrie sees from within, perhaps paradoxically, is external, empirical evidence of change in her relation to the physical world. Her brain, like Henry Fleming's, records this evidence and assesses her position accordingly. What she sees from without, perhaps equally paradoxically, is an abstract image of an intangibly "worsened" self, indicating a change in her relation to values that have no direct bearing on physical reality. Her conscience produces this image, but as Dreiser shows, its glass is neither smooth nor clear. While neither instructing the reader as to "which [image] to believe," as Mrs. Stowe would do, nor allowing Carrie a conscious solution to her own dilemma, the novelist undertakes to demonstrate how they interact, and which really determines Carrie's behavior.

Carrie's mental argument with her conscience (which Dreiser provides with a literal, quotable voice) is reminiscent in technique of many scenes in *Uncle Tom's Cabin,* and of the allegorized mental debate between "discretion" and "charity" in Roger Lawrence's mind at the beginning of *Watch and Ward.* As omniscient moderator of this debate, however, Dreiser exercises a different sort of control over his heroine's thoughts than either Stowe or James exercised. Mrs. Stowe simply enforces, through the voice of a conscience which actually constitutes the character's mind, a view or value preendorsed implicitly by the reader as well as explicitly by the author; and the early James and Howells tend to do the same. Dreiser, however, examines Carrie's conscience in its relation to responses made by other aspects of her mind to pressures other than moral. *Always* a "just and sapient counsellor" in the earlier fiction, a repository of absolute values, conscience is in Carrie a confused amalgam of "past environment, habit, convention." Her conscience is itself a product of environment, of her past exposure to conventional attitudes, in the same sense that her action—immoral according to her conscience—is the result of change in her environment. It represents to Carrie's mind and to Dreiser's narrative not divine truth, as it does in *Uncle Tom's Cabin,* but social opinion. The pressure of such opinion exists, as indeed conscience exists in Dreiser's fictive psychology. It is as real as the other forces with which the novelist is concerned. But it is not the dominant psychological "fact" of the situation.

Unsatisfied emotional cravings and the need for physical security are the dominant factors in Carrie's decision to accept Drouet's proposition. She does not really deliberate this decision any more than Henry Fleming deliberates his decision to run. It simply occurs, and neither through conscious opportunism nor through conscious sacrifice of values. Rather, like Maggie but in a more fully and clearly described way, she responds unconsciously to instinctual values of accommodation or survival. The moral impulse, absent in Maggie except (ironically of course) during the theater scene, makes itself felt in Carrie only infrequently, "when something else did not interfere." The pleasures and the "threats" of her new environment, which is now becoming habitual to her, gradually dim and usually screen out the voice of conscience. When it does penetrate her consciousness, these environmental pleasures and threats make effective answer. The "Counsel of Winter" (Dreiser's title for Chapter 10) replaces the counsel of a just and sapient conscience; the "voice of want"—of physical needs and emotional desires—replaces the voice of a moral guide. This new, or newly dominant, voice within her answers the questions posed by environment rather than those posed by conventional morality, and it does so without her conscious agency. In her occasional and increasingly feeble efforts to analyze the situation according to conscience, Carrie

> . . . had not the mind to get firm hold upon a definite truth. When she could not find her way out of the labyrinth of illogic which thought upon the subject created, she would turn away entirely.[8]

For Isabel Archer, the truth lies somewhere within the labyrinth, and to break out of it is to turn away from the problem. For Carrie, the labyrinthine complexities of introspective thought are by definition illogical and unrelated to the real problem. The implication is that "definite truth" in the moral sense does not exist. Carrie must therefore trust to her emotional impulses, and this is in accord with Dreiser's overall view of the mind and its relation to environment, which is very nearly the moral universe of the novel.

The mental state of another character receives Dreiser's close attention in a later passage dealing with another situation of moral conflict and choice. Once again the novelist is primarily interested in the interior mechanics of conflict and choice, the psychological facts underlying the operation—or the abrogation—of a moral principle. His treatment of this situation, however, reveals aspects of his fictive psychology not clearly apparent in the scene just described. Hurstwood, whose final deterioration Dreiser analyzes in the passage discussed in the Introduction, is, at this point, the middle-aged manager of a prosperous Chicago saloon. Although married, he has become interested in Carrie after he met her through Drouet, and has hopes of divorcing his wife and persuading her to marry him. Carrie is also attracted to Hurstwood, who represents possibilities for a more refined and expansive life than she has known with Drouet. (We recall that Pete in Crane's *Maggie* is also a bar manager, and that he represents to Maggie the possibility of escape from a restrictive environment.) Most of Hurstwood's property, however, is in his wife's name, and he is baffled as to how to get the divorce and enough money to go away with Carrie. As he makes his closing rounds at the saloon, he finds the safe open with the day's receipts, some ten thousand dollars, inside. Strongly tempted, he handles the money, then puts it back without locking the safe. Dreiser then writes:

> To those who have never wavered in conscience, the predicament of the individual whose mind is less strongly constituted and who trembles in the balance between duty and desire is scarcely appreciable, unless graphically portrayed. Those who have never heard that solemn voice of the ghostly clock which ticks with awful distinctness, "thou shalt," "thou shalt not," "thou shalt," "thou shalt not," are in no position to judge. Not alone in sensitive, highly organised natures is such a mental conflict possible. The dullest specimen of humanity, when drawn by desire toward evil, is recalled by a sense of right, which is proportionate in power and strength to his evil tendency. We must remember that it may not be a knowledge of right, for no knowledge of right is predicated of the animal's instinctive recoil at evil. Men are still led by instinct before they are regulated by knowledge. It is instinct which recalls the criminal—it is instinct (where highly organised reasoning is absent) which gives the criminal his feeling of danger, his fear of wrong.
>
> At every first adventure, then, into some untried evil, the mind wavers. The clock of thought ticks out its wish and its denial. To those who have never experienced such a mental dilemma, the following will appeal on the simple ground of revelation.
>
> When Hurstwood put the money back, his nature once again resumed its ease and daring. No one had observed him.

He was quite alone. No one could tell what he wished to do. He could work this thing out for himself. . . .

He took out the drawer again and lifted the bills. They were so smooth, so compact, so portable. How little they made, after all. He decided he would take them. Yes, he would. . . .

First he brought the bills and then the loose receipts of the day. He would take it all. He put the empty drawers back and pushed the iron door almost to, then stood beside it, meditating.

The wavering of a mind under such circumstances is an almost inexplicable thing, and yet it is absolutely true. Hurstwood could not bring himself to act definitely. He wanted to think about it—to ponder over it, to decide whether it were best. He was drawn by such a keen desire for Carrie, driven by such a state of turmoil in his own affairs that he thought constantly it would be best, and yet he wavered. He did not know what evil might result from it to him—how soon he might come to grief. The true ethics of the situation never once occurred to him, and never would have under any circumstances.

After he had all the money in the hand bag, a revulsion of feeling seized him. He would not do it—no! Think of what a scandal it would make. The police. They would be after him. He would have to fly, and where? Oh, the terror of being a fugitive from justice! He took out the two boxes and put all the money back. In his excitement he forgot what he was doing, and put the sums in the wrong boxes. As he pushed the door to he thought he remembered doing it wrong and opened the door again. There were the two boxes mixed.

He took them out and straightened the matter, but now the terror was gone. Why be afraid?

While the money was in his hand the lock clicked. It had sprung! Did he do it? He grabbed at the knob and pulled vigorously. It had closed. . . .

The moment he realised that the safe was locked for a surety, the sweat burst out upon his brow and he trembled violently. He looked about him and decided instantly. There was no delaying now.[9]

Just as the processes determining Carrie's behavior in the earlier scene require Dreiser's analytical attention if that behavior is to be understood, the processes underlying Hurstwood's predicament require both theoretical analysis and graphic portrayal if the dramatic situation is to be "appreciable," a valid link in the overall narrative sequence. The same is true of the passage from *Sister Carrie* in the Introduction—it constitutes the theoretical basis, analogous to the first two paragraphs here and to the longest paragraph in the passage from *McTeague,* from which Hurstwood's actual disintegration is subsequently narrated. Here, as there, Dreiser assumes the stance of a narrator-analyst empowered to reveal to the inexperienced the details of what such persons would not otherwise be able immediately to see. The "simple ground of revelation" itself is adequate justification for his analytical interest in Hurstwood's inner state, whereas scriptural revelation in *Uncle Tom's Cabin* makes such interest largely unnecessary to Mrs. Stowe.

Moral mechanics and mental mechanics are basically the same in this passage, but not in the sense in which we observed such fusion earlier. In *Uncle Tom's Cabin* and in the early fiction of James and Howells, mental process *is* moral reflex. In *Sister Carrie,* moral analysis has become altogether a matter of psychological analysis, an inverted fusion which we saw emerging in distinct but related forms in Howells's *A Hazard of New Fortunes* and Crane's *The Red Badge of Courage.*

Dreiser's theory of moral and mental mechanics is not the same as Norris's, although a basic similarity in the notion of instinctual struggle between the "desire toward evil" and the "sense of right" is clear. Norris's panther image is perhaps more graphic in its momentarily vivid detail than Dreiser's clock, but Dreiser's dramatic implementation of his image, like the object of the image itself, proceeds with a great deal more detached and measured regularity, both conceptually and linguistically. His notion of moral conflict as mental balance between opposed instincts seems to account for a case like McTeague's without limiting itself to it. By comparison with Hurstwood, who at this point is reasonably "sensitive" and "highly organised"—and quite successful in the Darwinian sense though nearing the turning point in his evolutionary fortunes—McTeague is "the dullest specimen of humanity." In him as well, however, essentially the same process occurs as goes on within Hurstwood's mind, despite Norris's reluctance to deal with the process as fully in dramatic terms as in terms of an archetypal abstraction. Dreiser addresses himself to an analytical point which is only implicit and not explained in *McTeague:* that what Norris calls an "unreasoned instinct of resistance" to evil, but also seems to imagine as a moral consciousness of more traditional clarity, may indeed be something innate and wholly unconscious. In both writers, therefore, a moral theory based on instinctive reaction, which is divorced from considerations of a spiritual or divine reality, and placed firmly within a framework of psychological—sometimes physiological—analysis, nevertheless attempts to account for interior experience as comprehensively and as enclosedly as a moral system such as Mrs. Stowe's.

Thus, Dreiser makes no attempt to dispense with the abstract vocabulary of moral theory here to the extent that he does in delineating the mechanics of Hurstwood's physical and mental degeneration later on. "Evil" and "right," the moral imperatives "thou shalt" and "thou shalt not" complete with their Biblical forms—these are intrinsic to the bond between moral and psychological analysis established in the first paragraph. It is not now God, any more than Carrie's conscience represents the voice of God, who utters the commandments "thou shalt," "thou shalt not." It is a mental clock, an instrument of pure mechanism, whatever analogy to the traditional function of the soul Dreiser may intend in the word "ghostly." The novelist is not quite as prepared here as he is in the passage about Hurstwood's decline to account for everything in literal biochemical or mechanical terms; the clock remains, in this theoretical portion of the passage, more figurative than the "poisons in the blood" which determine Hurstwood's decay. It is a clock none the less; the imagery of fluidity and conscious flow which we found increasingly abundant in James's fiction as he progressed, and the mixture of such images with others of animal and mechanical instinct in Crane's *Red Badge,* have now become pervasively the imagery of mechanism in *Sister Carrie.*

The mechanism of the safe becomes identified with the operation of Hurstwood's mind as the scene develops itself from the theoretical base of the opening paragraphs. Just before this passage, a "voice" in his consciousness says (and Dreiser quotes it formally), "The safe is open. . . . The lock has not yet sprung." And then it asks, "What about it?" The rest of the passage deals with the mental mechanisms by which the lock *is* eventually sprung and Hurstwood's decision taken. As in *McTeague,* emphasis falls on the behavioral result of a mental process: McTeague kisses Trina "before he knew it"; Carrie finds herself already established in Drouet's apartment before she consciously considers the problem; Hurstwood wonders, "Did [I] do it?" after the mechanism of his mind and the mechanism of the safe have simultaneously operated, or "sprung." After, when Hurstwood and Carrie are in Montreal having fled Chicago together, Dreiser describes his mind as "working like a key-board of a telephone station." The novelist neither emphasizes nor develops the simile to the extent that he does the clock image. Yet it seems to confirm a tendency toward increasingly basic mechanical imagery for the operation of mental process as this novel develops, comparable to the tendency toward increasingly prevalent imagery of mental flow as James's career develops. The character's mind has become a morally neutral, purely mechanical control center, divorced even further from the role of conscience than when it was seen as the mental clock, and capable of channeling but not of controlling the nature of the information it receives from instinctual or sensory sources.

Hurstwood's meditation as he stands before the open safe and before a supposedly open choice, is not a process of measured introspection resulting in clear inward sight of the sort emphasized in James and Howells. Although he consciously "wanted to think about it—to ponder over it, to decide whether it were best," he actually goes through a process of automatic action and reaction among thoroughly practical contingencies. What is best is what seems most likely to gain him Carrie, and toward this he is driven by sexual desire and emotional turmoil. What is evil is what may concretely result to worsen his physical situation, pursuit by police rather than his own flight from abstract justice. His terror, like Basil March's, is more the "feeling of danger" than the "fear of wrong," and we recall that at the end of the first paragraph Dreiser seems to equate the latter with the former. The true ethics of the situation, which may exist for Dreiser but which he elaborates no more than he comments on the definite truth which Carrie's mind cannot grasp in the earlier sequence, simply do not enter.

In *Roderick Hudson,* the hero speculated that moral and mental "currents" were subtly intertwined within the overall flow of human consciousness, adding with regard to the particular patterns that such currents might develop in particular situations: "It all depends on circumstances." Here Dreiser demonstrates Roderick's theory, adapting it to his controlling conception of mechanism rather than flow, but also extending the notion of psychological dependence on circumstance. For Hurstwood, as dramatically revealed rather than as theoretically considered, there is nothing *but* circumstance.

In Mrs. Stowe's fiction, and in James's and Howells's fiction at the outset of their careers, we saw the "strange law of mind" either set aside as irrelevant to the main concerns of the novel, or tentatively approached before being rejected as subject matter inaccessible to the novelist. What Mrs. Stowe found prohibitively "strange" remains for Dreiser "almost inexplicable." But because he finds it "absolutely true"—possessed of the reality which for Mrs. Stowe resided only in Christian morality—Dreiser's primary responsibility as a novelist is to explain psychological process in the course of representing real experience. This he does, according to his conceptual lights, methodically and indeed sometimes tediously, but faithfully as well in a manner suggesting (without in the least resembling) James's final artistic faith in the drama of the mind.

Afterword

Sheldon Corthell, a character in Norris's *The Pit,* says in that novel during a conversation about literature that "the novel of the future is going to be a novel without a love story." In observing the emergence, over this period, of the novel of the future as it becomes the novel of the present and supplants the novel of the past, our concern has been with psychological representation and not with sentimental conventions as such. We have seen James pursue his interest in the movement of the mind as the stuff of drama to the point that the religion of consciousness becomes his esthetic creed. We have watched Howells develop from an inability to represent the "fastnesses" of the mind to an explicit curiosity regarding its intricacies, and finally to a partial ability to represent the moral and environmental pressures upon it. We have seen Crane move from a theoretical interest toward dramatic capability with the material of thought, the substance from which the crucial scenes in *The Red Badge of Courage* are formed. We have witnessed Norris and Dreiser embark on careers in a new century with works which seem to embody the developments reflected in the work of these other novelists.

Yet Corthell's prediction is of interest at this point, for it suggests one of the many relations existing between changes observed in the foregoing chapters and those—often observable in the same materials—contributing in various other ways to "the rise of realism" in American fiction. My purpose is not to document this relation at length, any more than it is to catalog the possible correspondences between literary and theoretical psychology implied by the quotation from William James in Chapter 2. Such correspondences there certainly are, and particularly between the fictive and formal psychologies of Henry and William James, but how they arrive is a much more complicated matter, and I am convinced on the basis of a certain amount of labor that they are anything but neatly one-to-one. My purpose is, however, by way of concluding this book, to suggest how the current of change we have observed interpenetrates with others when we step back from our intensive analysis to gain a more general view. Just as when a deep river is surveyed from altitude we see its currents intermingle, so the literary changes we have observed blend "like water into water" with others comprising the mysterious complexity and inviolability of the total and individual work of art. We do not lose sight of what we have seen at close range by stepping back. We do find, however, that the "conclusion" of an investigation into these phenomena creates prospects on other changes and relationships, and fortunately so.

The question behind Corthell's remark, what "the novel of the future" is to be or is to have as its organizing principle *instead* of a love story, finds its answer, regarding our period, in the area of fictive psychology. Howells moves from the conventionally defined (however abortive) love story in *A Chance Acquaintance* to his tentatively psychological treatment of "modern love" in *A Modern Instance*. Then he proceeds from his theoretical criticism of sentimental conventions, voiced through the Reverend Mr. Sewell, in *The Rise of Silas Lapham,* to his dramatic relegation of such conventions to minor plot lines in *A Hazard of New Fortunes*. In both cases he turns increasingly to psychological analysis at the expense of considerations of romantic role. James's fiction shows a similar if more linear development, although he concerns himself less with explicitly attacking the conventions of the love story than with expanding the circumference of his characters' interior experience first against and then beyond their constraining limits. The love story latent within *The Ambassadors* necessarily remains so, and has little to do with the focus or structure of that work, while James's psychological preoccupations have "everything" to do with such matters. Crane's *Maggie* is an ironic grotesque of a love story rather than a total departure from any artistic concern whatsoever with its conventions, and *The Red Badge of Courage* is perhaps a novel of the future only by default, since it lacks female characters altogether. Yet the same intensification of psychological interest and representational effort at the expense of abstractly formulated roles is apparent in the difference between these two works by Crane. Despite its date (1903), *The Pit* is more dependent on elements of the conventional love story than is Norris's earlier *McTeague*. But Dreiser's *Sister Carrie* may be viewed as fulfilling Corthell's prophecy before it was made.

Sister Carrie deals with romantic attachment of a sort as well as with sexual attraction, and as heroine Carrie is not completely without the vestiges of conventional roots, as her audible though ineffectual conscience suggests. In a sense much more important to the novel's overall development, however, Carrie is portrayed as outside of the relationships on which the conventional love plot depends. She is "alone" throughout (Dreiser uses the term insistently), and those who find in her final solitude a significant element of moral retribution forget that she is alone in scene after scene, not only in the literal dramatic sense but in terms of Dreiser's definition of her essential identity as well. However her affections may be engaged in relationships that would correspond to the love plot in a more traditional framework, the voice of need—physical, material, emotional (in a physiological rather than a romantic sense)—determines her course of action. Love has no power over reality in the world of this novel. Conversely, however Kitty's affections are engaged in *A Chance Acquaintance,* the unrepresented moral insight attending her innocence prevents her from a course of action which would contravene romantic conventions. An ideal of love, which Arbuton fails to measure up to, does exert a controlling power over the facts of this fictive world.

Thus, as Carrie gravitates away from Drouet and toward Hurstwood, she is "busy adjusting her thoughts and feelings to newer conditions, and [is] not in danger of suffering disturbing pangs"—moral *or* sentimental—"from either quarter." Her instincts are in accord with Dreiser's view of reality, just as the moral insights governing earlier characters accord with a view of reality such as Mrs. Stowe's. Her adaptive psychology helps her cope with environmental facts, and the lack of moral orientation in her inward life has had no basic impact on her outward experience or final position. She has no analytical understanding of this; the labyrinth is too deep for her. But just as Hurstwood degenerates—fails in the Darwinian sense—through a process involving poisons in the blood, Carrie succeeds through an almost equally biochemical resilience. She is therefore as innocent in Dreiser's terms as Tom or Nora or Kitty in Stowe's or James's or Howells's terms. Through her interior responses to the pressures of reality—responses which Dreiser, like James, takes as his primary task to reveal, to "graphically portray"—she fulfills inexorable environmental law, just as our earliest heroines fulfilled, through unrevealed and perhaps unportrayable responses to the abstract requirements of reality conceived in a different way, inflexible moral law.

What Carrie has been blindly seeking and still vaguely longs for at the end of the novel is an ideal condition which Dreiser envisions as still far off in the future of humanity. In this condition, instinct will be a new kind of reason, unencumbered by habitual illusions about the nature of experience, and perfectly "aligned by nature with the forces of life." Free will in such a future will be the complete understanding of the brain as an adaptive mechanism, and the free use of its capacities (physiologically circumscribed though *these* may be) in the interest of evolutionary progress. Carrie's inward life is simply an incident in the progress of man as a "creature of incalculable variety"—the very antithesis of a conventional type—toward this ideal. Yet in that life and in her final isolation, as in Strether's in *The Ambassadors,* we find the psychological grounding not simply for an individual characterization, but for an entire fictive action.

Thus, the twentieth century opens to American fiction, and the novel of the future passes into the present on its way to the past. The new modes of thought we have watched become possible amid the shifting terrain of new literary geographies seem in many ways older and less possible to us now. The conditions which created them, and which for a time entrusted to them the real and the true, have themselves been largely recreated. They continue to underly, none the less, and to some extent still inform, our own efforts to reinterpret the real through the lens of the mind.

Notes

INTRODUCTION

1. Excluding Mark Twain from this group requires a word of explanation. Fictive psychology is no less an element of his art than it is of any of the other writers', and the problem of dramatizing the inward life is by no means absent from *Huckleberry Finn,* as both Henry Nash Smith and Richard Poirier have shown. Yet Twain's main energies as a force of change in American fiction seem to be focused in other directions, such as toward forging a fundamentally new colloquial style. Huck Finn's speech is of course Twain's chosen device for conveying Huck's thought. But the way Huck speaks is nevertheless more important than the way he thinks. Twain's manipulation of an explicit voice is more essential to the movement and the meaning of the novel than is his conception and representation of an interior process. See Henry Nash Smith, *Mark Twain: The Development of a Writer* (Cambridge, Mass., 1962); Richard Poirier, *A World Elsewhere: The Place of Style in American Literature* (New York, 1966); and Richard Bridgman, *The Colloquial Style in America* (New York, 1966).
2. Novels closer in time to the early 1870's, when movement away from such practice becomes clearly apparent, might serve the

same purpose. But few seem as artistically comparable to James's or Howells's work and as usefully typical as does Mrs. Stowe's. As for Hawthorne, Melville, or even Poe, earlier writers with indisputable psychological interests, their very relevance—within a larger historical frame—to matters psychological in nineteenth-century American literature more broadly viewed excludes them here. That relevance is another story, though an absorbing one, for another book. More immediately, each of these authors is in some way an *un*conventional artist regarding the practices which bind the early writing of James and Howells to conventions effectively exemplified in *Uncle Tom's Cabin.* Hawthorne's fiction in particular, despite its psychological sophistication, offers a point of departure less useful to us than Mrs. Stowe's because it is unrepresentative of the point from which James and Howells appear to depart. Hawthorne requires special consideration, such as that found in Frederick Crews's *The Sins of the Fathers: Hawthorne's Psychological Themes* (New York, 1966), and the same may be said of Melville and Poe.

3. Harriet Beecher Stowe, *Uncle Tom's Cabin* (Boston, 1852), vol. I, pp. 172–73.
4. Theodore Dreiser, *Sister Carrie* (New York, 1900), pp. 360–62.
5. Warner Berthoff, *The Ferment of Realism: American Literature, 1884–1919* (New York, 1965).

CHAPTER I

1. James made numerous changes for the 1878 edition [see B. R. McElderry, Jr., "Henry James's Revision of *Watch and Ward,*" *Modern Language Notes* (November, 1952), pp. 457–61], but none of these alterations produced any real shift in conceptual foundations or narrative proportions. All passages discussed here are virtually the same in the 1878 text, from which I quote, as they are in the 1871 version.
2. Harriet Beecher Stowe, *Uncle Tom's Cabin* (Boston, 1852), vol. I, pp. 229–30.
3. *Ibid.*, vol. II, p. 253.
4. *Ibid.*, pp. 187, 225.
5. *Ibid.*, pp. 214–15.

6. *Ibid.*, vol. I, pp. 80–82.
7. Henry James, *Watch and Ward* (Boston, 1878), p. 8.
8. *Ibid.*, p. 10.
9. *Ibid.*, pp. 206–07.
10. *Ibid.*, p. 212.
11. *Ibid.*, p. 171.
12. William Dean Howells, *A Chance Acquaintance* (Boston, 1873), pp. 150–53.
13. We learn certain of Kitty's thoughts only because Howells tells us that she "had written home" about them (see p. 2), and Chapter 6 is epistolary narrative throughout. In *Watch and Ward,* Nora's first active response to the crisis precipitated by her discovery of Lawrence's intentions, is a letter written to him (see p. 173).
14. Stowe, *Uncle Tom's Cabin,* vol. II, p. 253; James, *Watch and Ward,* p. 170; Howells, *A Chance Acquaintance,* p. 242.
15. Howells, *A Chance Acquaintance,* p. 251.
16. Leon Edel, "Introduction" to *Watch and Ward* (London: Rupert Hart-Davis, 1960), p. 10.
17. Howells, *A Chance Acquaintance,* p. 153.

CHAPTER 2

1. Leon Edel, *Henry James: The Conquest of London, 1870–1883* (London: Rupert Hart-Davis, 1962), p. 40.
2. James revised *Roderick Hudson,* as he did nearly all his works, for the 1907–9 New York Edition. As in the case of *Watch and Ward,* revision had no fundamental impact on the psychological assumptions and techniques in question. I quote, in this chapter, from the New York Edition texts of *The Portrait of a Lady* (vols. III and IV) and *The Ambassadors* (vols. XXI and XXII) as well from *Roderick* (vol. I), for the reader's convenience in view of my frequent references to James's prefaces to these novels.
3. Henry James, *Roderick Hudson* (New York, 1907), pp. vi–vii.
4. *Ibid.*, p. xvii.
5. *Ibid.*
6. *Ibid.*, pp. 87–88.
7. Henry James, *Watch and Ward* (Boston, 1878), p. 147.
8. In his original preface to this novel, Holmes suggests his priorities

as a novelist with certain psychological concerns: "I have attempted to show the successive evolution of some inherited qualities in the character of Myrtle Hazard [his heroine], not so obstrusively as to disturb the narrative. . . ." Later in the novel itself he remarks on certain complexities in Myrtle's mental life: "It is not for us [i.e., novelists], who only tell what happened, to solve these mysteries. . . ."

9. Oliver Wendell Holmes, *The Works of Oliver Wendell Holmes* (Boston, 1892), vol. VI, p. 117.
10. James, *Roderick Hudson,* p. 175.
11. *Ibid.,* pp. 314–15.
12. Henry James, *The Portrait of a Lady* (New York, 1908), vol. I, p. xv.
13. *Ibid.,* p. xx.
14. *Ibid.,* pp. xx–xxi.
15. *Ibid.,* vol. II, p. 165.
16. *Ibid.,* pp. 186–88.
17. *Ibid.,* pp. 188–91.
18. William James, *The Principles of Psychology* (New York, 1890), vol. I, p. 255.
19. Henry James, *The Ambassadors* (New York, 1909), vol. I, p. vi.
20. *Ibid.,* pp. xii–xiii.
21. See pp. 106–8 in *Roderick Hudson,* and pp. 195–97 in vol. I of *The Ambassadors.* I am indebted for the suggestion of this comparison to Jonathan R. Grandine, a former student whose unpublished essay on James I have found valuably stimulating.
22. James, *The Ambassadors,* vol. I, pp. 195–97.
23. *Ibid.,* pp. 217–18.
24. I am indebted to Mr. Grandine's essay for the supporting references in this paragraph.
25. James, *The Ambassadors,* vol. II, p. 75.

CHAPTER 3

1. William Dean Howells, *A Modern Instance* (Boston, 1882), p. 45.
2. *Ibid.,* p. 511.
3. *Ibid.,* p. 69.

4. *Ibid.*, pp. 79–81.
5. *Ibid.*, p. 96.
6. Henry James, *Roderick Hudson* (New York, 1907), p. 141.
7. William Dean Howells, *The Rise of Silas Lapham* (Boston, 1885), p. 287.
8. *Ibid.*, pp. 67–68.
9. *Ibid.*, pp. 463–67.
10. William Dean Howells, *A Hazard of New Fortunes* (New York, 1890), vol. II, p. 132.
11. *Ibid.*, pp. 137–38.
12. Dorothea Krook, *The Ordeal of Consciousness in Henry James* (Cambridge, 1962).
13. F. O. Matthiessen, *Henry James: The Major Phase* (New York, 1944), chapter 6.
14. Howells, *A Hazard of New Fortunes,* vol. II, pp. 318–19.

CHAPTER 4

1. Stephen Crane, *The Work of Stephen Crane,* ed. by Wilson Follett (New York, 1963), vol. X, p. 159. Contains a loose paraphrase from *Isaiah.*
2. Quoted by R. W. Stallman, *Stephen Crane: A Biography* (New York: George Braziller, 1968), p. 78.
3. Crane, *Work,* vol. X, p. 189.
4. *Ibid.*, pp. 171–72.
5. Crane, *Work,* vol. I, pp. 30–31.
6. *Ibid.*, p. 149.
7. Henry James, *The Portrait of a Lady* (New York, 1908), vol. II, p. 436.
8. Crane, *Work,* vol. I, p. 35.
9. *Ibid.*, p. 74.
10. *Ibid.*, p. 82.
11. *Ibid.*, pp. 81–82.
12. *Ibid.*, p. 86.
13. *Ibid.*, pp. 159–60.
14. *Ibid.*, pp. 160.
15. *Ibid.*, pp. 196–99.

CHAPTER 5

1. Frank Norris, [*Works*] (Garden City, New York, 1928), vol. VIII, p. 23.
2. Norris, [*Works*], vol. VII, pp. 167–68.
3. Larzer Ziff, *The American 1890s: Life and Times of a Lost Generation* (New York: The Viking Press, 1966), p. 258.
4. Norris, [*Works*], vol. VIII, pp. 25–27.
5. Quoted by Donald Pizer, "Evolutionary Ethical Dualism in Frank Norris's *Vandover and the Brute* and *McTeague*," *Publications of the Modern Language Association* (December, 1961), p. 554.
6. Theodore Dreiser, *Sister Carrie* (New York, 1900), p. 101.
7. *Ibid.*, pp. 103–04.
8. *Ibid.*, p. 105.
9. *Ibid.*, pp. 286–89.

Index

(*References in boldface type indicate major discussions.*)